D0515602

INDIANA

Lake Michigan

Hammond • • Gary

Elkhart •

South Bend •

20

30

Fort Wayne •

65

Huntington •

Kankakee R.

Tippecanoe R.

24

Logansport •

Wabash R.

31

Marion •

27

69

Missisinewa R.

West Lafayette •
Lafayette •

Kokomo •

Frankfort •

Muncie •

White R.

41

Anderson •

Franklin Township (1,257 ft) ▲

Crawfordsville •

74

36

70

Richmond •

231

Eel R.

Indianapolis

Wabash R.

70

65

Brookville Lake

Terre Haute •

Greensburg •

Columbus •

74

421

Bloomington •

Monroe Lake

50

Hoosier Nat'l Forest

231

White R.

Bedford •

Madison •

Ohio R.

Vincennes •

Shoals •

65

Hoosier

150

New Albany

Patoka Lake

41

National

64

Forest

Evansville •

Ohio R.

INDIANA BY ROAD

CELEBRATE THE STATES
INDIANA

Marlene Targ Brill

BENCHMARK BOOKS

MARSHALL CAVENDISH
NEW YORK

Acknowledgments

Nonfiction writers often depend on the kindness of others for much of their information. Some people who generously contributed to Indiana were Dr. Robert Taylor Jr., Indiana Historical Society; Ruth Brown, Limberlost State Historical Site; Nancy Wolfe, Indiana Junior Historical Society; Nick Clark, Prophetstown State Park Foundation; Richard Day, Indiana Territory State Historic Site; Rodney Richardson, Angel Mounds; Eric Mundell, Indiana Historical Society; Marybeth Morgan, Indiana Department of Education; Barbara Mummey, Turkey Run State Park; Linda Crawford, Circus City Festival; and Jim Holland, Roachdale. Special thanks go to Raymond Bial, Hoosier photojournalist; Felice Glazier, Noblesville Public Schools; and Dena and Harry Targ, Purdue University.

Benchmark Books
Marshall Cavendish Corporation
99 White Plains Road
Tarrytown, New York 10591-9001

Copyright © 1997 by Marshall Cavendish Corporation

Library of Congress Cataloging-in-Publication Data
Brill, Marlene Targ.
Indiana / Marlene Targ Brill.
p.   cm. — (Celebrate the states)
Includes bibliographical references and index.
Summary: Discusses the history of Indiana, as well as its present, its people, and its places of interest.
ISBN 0-7614-0147-4 (lib. bdg.)
1. Indiana—Juvenile literature. [1. Indiana.] I. Title. II. Series.
F526.3.B75   1997   977.2—dc20   96-26369   CIP   AC

Maps and graphics supplied by Oxford Cartographers, Oxford, England

Photo research by Ellen Barrett Dudley

Cover photo: Odyssey/Chigago, Kevin O. Mooney

The photographs in this book are used by permission and through the courtesy of: Unicorn Stock Photos: Robert W. Ginn, 6-7, 17, 77; Mary Stadtfeld, 10-11; Ted Rose, 15, 129; Andre Jenny, 52-53, 115, 117, 140; D. & I. MacDonald, 65; Sohm/Chromosohm, back cover. Odyssey/Chicago/Russel Gordon: 13. Photo Researchers, Inc.: Ray Coleman, 16; Farrell Grehan, 59; Charles W. Mann, 123 (left); Tim Davis, 126. © James P. Rowan: 20, 22, 29, 38, 86-87, 109, 112, 131. Indiana Dunes National Lakeshore: 25. Indianapolis Museum of Art: 26-27. The National Park Service/George Rogers Clark NHP: 31. Nawrocki Stock Photo, Inc.: 34. Indiana Historical Society Library: neg. # KCT 11, 35; neg. # C2318, 40; neg. # C4363, 43; neg. # C5825, 46; neg. # 207580F, 89; neg. # C2140, 137. Calumet Regional Archives, Indiana University Northwest, Gary Public Library Collection: 48. Hohenberger MSS., Manuscripts Department, Lilly Library, Indiana University: 50. UPI/Corbis-Bettmann: 56, 91, 92, 95, 102, 133, 134 (top & bottom), 136. Daybreak Imagery/Richard Day: 63, 68-69, 85, 123 (right). Valparaiso Popcorn Festival: 64. The Image Bank: Santi Visalli, 67; J.H. (Pete) Carmichael, 104-105; Marvin E. Newman, 114. © Steve Baker/Highlight Imagery: 71, 79, 83. Ethnic Expo: 75. Indiana University Photographic Services: 81. Archive Photos: 82 (left & right). Collection of the Indiana State Museum and Historic Sites: 94. Reuters/Corbis-Bettmann: 97. Magnum Photos, Inc., © 1995 Dennis Stock: 99. Indianapolis Motor Speedway/Indy 500 Photos: 100. Raymond Bial: 111. Circus City Festival, Inc.: 121. Allen County Public Library: 132.

Printed in Italy

1   3   5   6   4   2

CONTENTS

INDIANA IS . . .

Indiana has a peaceful and varied landscape . . .

"We have the most beautiful woods and plants—ferns and bayberry."
—Jane Stuart, Harrison County buffalo farmer

"From sand dunes to streams running in limestone canyons . . . the natural . . . wonders of Indiana come alive."
—William Forgey, Merrillville author and outdoorsman

. . . and an exciting history.

"My father kindled the first fire at Detroit . . . thence extended their line . . . down the Ohio to the mouth of the Wabash."
—Little Turtle, Miami chief, 1795

"I am a woman who came from the cotton fields of the South . . . I promoted myself into the business of manufacturing hair goods. . . . I have built my own factory on my own ground."
—Madam C. J. Walker, the nation's
first black millionaire, Indianapolis

People here have their differences . . .

"The belief that the Calumet [region] is not really 'Indiana' has sometimes taken extreme forms. . . . In 1935, a bill [came] before the state legislature to establish the county as the forty-ninth state."
—Robert Taylor, historian, *Indiana: A New Historical Guide*

"No one ever represented the thinking and . . . heart of Hoosierland better than Bill Jenner [U.S. senator, 1954–1958]. He is . . . suspicious of strangers and fearful of new ideas."

—Irving Liebowitz, author of *My Indiana*

. . . but they stick together.

"High school basketball has connected the industrial cities of the northwest to the urban center in Indianapolis to the . . . farm communities in the southern part of the state."

—Barry Temkin, reporter

"There's a sense of youth, small-town pride, and a strong feeling of community."

—Raymond Bial, Seymour-born children's author and photographer

They are proud to call Indiana their home.

"My hometown—not just another pretty place!"

—Garfield the cat, Muncie

Moreover, Indiana is middle America. Its people value the simple things in life—their small towns, varied products, beautiful countryside, and famous sons and daughters. Indiana's contrasts will surprise you. But so will its down-home treasures. This is Indiana's story.

1 NATURAL WONDERS

Ogle Lake

About ten thousand years ago, four ice slabs, called glaciers, crept along North America's central region. As they moved, the mile-thick glaciers flattened mountains, ground rocks, and carved riverbeds. These changes shaped the land we call Indiana.

HEART OF THE MIDWEST

"Indiana is not Out West or Way Down East or Up North or South in Dixie," wrote Indiana author George Ade. "Rather, it's smack in the middle of America."

And that's what people from Indiana like. Many residents believe their central spot in the nation's heartland makes them special. People pride themselves on their sense of balance, fair play, and strong middle-of-the-road beliefs. Their state motto, "Crossroads of America," describes Indiana's central location along highways, railroad lines, and water routes. But these words also express the pride residents feel as Middle Americans.

Indiana is the smallest of the twelve midwestern states. With about 36,000 square miles, the state ranks thirty-eighth in size. Indiana is considered a northern state, yet its tip extends into the South. "The glaciers ended here [in southern Indiana] and left the area with caves and sinkholes," said farmer Jane Stuart. "This place is where southern and northern plants meet."

The stubby, boot-shaped state divides into three regions: northern, central, and southern.

Northern Indiana. The north is lake country. About four hundred lakes flow through Indiana's rolling farmland. Lake Michigan—and its forty-five miles of Indiana shoreline—is the most striking natural feature of the region. Lake winds and waves wash rocks ashore and grind them into sand. Strong currents push sand from the lake bottom, forming peaceful sandy beaches and the largest sand mountains, or dunes, in North America.

At 123 feet high, Mount Baldy is the biggest dune. Yet winds can blow the sand mountain almost four feet each year. Today Mount

Mount Baldy overlooks Lake Michigan and a nearby power plant.

Baldy is burying an entire oak forest. Hikers claim they hear "singing sand" from its movement when the wind is right.

Inland from the sandy peaks are patches of fertile flatland and wetland. Thick forests of white pine, cedar, oak, and maple cover the northern quarter of the state. These trees are home to many migrating birds, such as bobwhites, chickadees, warblers, and herring gulls. Foxes, deer, beavers, skunks, mink, and dragonflies play under the trees' sheltering leaves.

Nature lovers especially like Pinhook Bog. Bogs are giant shallow clay bowls that were carved by glaciers and now trap pools of water. At Pinhook, plants grow thick on top of the waterlogged ground. Some of them even eat insects! Children love to jump on the bog to make the mossy ground jiggle.

Central Indiana. Central Indiana is good farm country. The region is called the Till Plains for its rich mixture of gravel and clay soil. Grain and livestock farms stretch as far as the eye can see. License plates that read AMBER WAVES OF GRAIN celebrate the importance of farming to this major corn- and wheat-growing state.

"I am much pleased with this country," wrote William Henry Harrison of central Indiana in 1801. "Nothing can exceed its beauty and fertility."

Only a few rolling hills and winding roads break up the mostly flat farmland. About every fifty miles, however, a clump of trees rises unexpectedly from the open land. Once hardwood forests spread across 90 percent of the area. Then settlers cleared the land and tilled the soil under. Now less than 13 percent of Indiana is forest.

"Indiana was a wild region with many bears and wild animals in

White-tailed deer graze on cornstalks in a farmer's field.

BUG-EATING PLANTS

Did you know that some plants eat insects? Three species of carnivorous plants live in Pinhook Bog.

Pitcher plants send water through tubes with hairy linings. When insects come to drink the water or lay eggs in it, they are trapped by the spiny hairs. The bugs rot and are absorbed into the plant.

Sundews have flowers that are smaller than your little fingernail. The flowers form sugary-tasting droplets that attract insects. But the droplets are sticky. Insects get stuck and become a meal for the sundew.

Then there is the bladderwort. This tiny plant has ten to twenty hollow balls that are slit in the center and hold water. Hairs inside the balls detect motion in the water. When a thirsty insect crawls into one of the balls, the hairs clamp down, locking the bug inside.

Indiana is a garden
Where the seeds of peace have grown,
Where each tree, and vine, and flower
Has a beauty all its own
  —from the state poem, "Indiana," by Arthur Mapes

the woods," remembered President Abraham Lincoln. "My father settled in an unbroken forest; and the clearing away of surplus woods was the great task at once."

Southern Indiana. In southern Indiana, wave-shaped hills and lowlands escaped the crushing glaciers and much of the farmers' plow. Today, scenic mountains with hidden caves snake

Lake Michigan

Hammond • •Gary

South Bend• •Elkhart

Kankakee R.

Tippecanoe R.

Fort Wayne•

•Huntington

Logansport• *Wabash R.*

Marion•

West Lafayette• Kokomo•

Lafayette•

•Muncie

Frankfort• *Mississinewa R.*

White R.

Crawfordsville• •Anderson

Franklin Township (1,257 ft)▲

Eel R.

Indianapolis Richmond•

Wabash R.

Terre Haute

Brookville Lake

•Greensburg

Bloomington• •Columbus

Monroe Lake

White R.

Bedford•

•Madison

Ohio R.

Vincennes• •Shoals

Patoka Lake New Albany

Evansville• *Ohio R.*

LAND AND WATER

through many untouched regions. Wyandotte Caves form the largest underground rooms in the world. The earth is filled with limestone and has oil and mineral deposits for mining.

Of the twenty-one state parks, the most striking run through Hoosier National Forest, from Bloomington to the Ohio River. Deer, coyote, badgers, opossums, owls, hawks, ferrets, foxes, and bears live in the wooded hills. Mineral springs, deep valleys, and ragged ridges attract vacationers and artists. The beauty of Brown County, one of nine counties in the forest, inspired the poet James Whitcomb Riley to write "Ain't God Good to Indiana?"

WATERWAYS TO THE WORLD

Rivers and lakes helped make Indiana the "Crossroads of America." Lake Michigan had a big effect on the way northern Indiana developed. Shorelike harbors opened Indiana to the Atlantic Ocean and beyond through the Great Lakes and the Saint Lawrence Seaway. Burns Waterway Harbor, on the southern tip of Lake Michigan, became Indiana's only industrial harbor not located along the Ohio River. Major industries and import-export businesses started here. This lakefront commercial strip was named the Calumet region after the bordering Grand Calumet and Little Calumet Rivers.

The most celebrated Indiana waterway, however, is the Wabash River. Countless songs and poems sing its praises. The most famous is the state song, "On the Banks of the Wabash, Far Away," by Paul Dresser.

The Wabash forms the boundary between the northern and central regions. It then runs southwest across the state to Terre

Each fall Tippecanoe County holds the Feast of the Hunters' Moon, an eighteenth-century French fair. Costumed pioneers canoe down the Wabash River to meet traders, soldiers, musicians, Native American dancers, and craftspeople.

Haute and southward into the Ohio River, shaping the state's western boundary with Illinois. The Ohio River separates Indiana from Kentucky to the south. The Wabash and Ohio Rivers played key roles in Native American and French settlement, as well as in early steamboat travel.

"The river draws him to it like a magnet, and on its banks he will stand for hours, simply watching the water glide past," wrote William Wilson in his novel *The Wabash*.

Most Indiana rivers drain into the Wabash. The White River runs southwest and meets the Wabash north of Mount Carmel. Other major branches of the Wabash are the Mississinewa, Tippecanoe, and Salamonie. These and several low-level streams fan throughout most of Indiana. Some travel southwesterly all the way to the Mississippi River and so into the Gulf of Mexico.

Indiana's canals linked rivers to improve shipping and travel. Small towns sprang up along these canal routes before train travel. At first, horse-drawn canal boats and flatboats carried goods and people downriver. Later, steamboats, which ran with or against the current, made river travel a booming success. Today, the Sugar Creek Canoe Race in Crawfordsville and the Madison Regatta honor the state's early boating days.

THE SEASONS

Indiana residents have an old saying: "If you don't like the weather in Indiana, wait five minutes."

Four distinct seasons determine how much time Indiana residents, or Hoosiers, spend outdoors and what farmers plant. Indiana's hot, muggy summers are well suited for growing tobacco and fruit, and its cold, snowy winters are ideal for snowmobiling. In between, the seasonal colors of autumn and spring lure hikers, bikers, and nature lovers outdoors.

In general, the weather can be humid, rainy, cloudy, or windy

Fourteen miles of the Whitewater Canal, which first attracted people and produce to eastern Indiana, is now a state historic site.

at any time of the year. But the climate can vary greatly between the north and the south within each season. One December traveler bundled herself in an overcoat and boots to weather Merrillville's icy streets and twenty-degree temperatures. The next day she headed south and roasted under New Harmony's sunny, sixty-degree sky.

Heavy rainstorms across Indiana flatlands have always been dangerous because they are often followed by severe floods. In 1884, Clara Barton launched the first Red Cross flood relief program in Evansville after floodwater soaked the river town. Over the years, floods have destroyed Lake Michigan shoreline and town streets along the Ohio River.

Rain and melting snow often fill the three rivers of Fort Wayne.

In March 1982, they spilled over, causing one of the state's worst floods ever. Over fifty thousand volunteers, mainly schoolchildren, stuffed and piled one million sandbags along eight miles of flood walls. The sight of so many children coming together captured the nation's attention. Reporters called the heroic teamwork the "children's crusade."

PRESERVING THE BEST OF INDIANA

Indiana has a long history of citizens working to better the environment. One of the most famous was Massachusetts-born John Chapman. About 1800, Chapman decided that "fruit is next to religion." He traveled westward carrying a flour sack filled with apple, plum, and cherry seeds, planting and preaching along the way. Orchards bloomed wherever the shoeless man with the tin-pan hat hiked, earning Chapman the nickname Johnny Appleseed.

From 1838 until his death in 1847, Chapman wandered through Indiana. He planted one of his biggest orchards in Fort Wayne. Today, Chapman's grave site near Fort Wayne is called Johnny Appleseed Memorial Park. Every September, people remember him with a festival bearing his name.

In 1916 there was a great uproar over land. State lawmakers threatened to sell dunes property for industry. Citizens fought back with the "Save the Dunes" movement. Seven years later, the state bought the lakefront land for a park. Still, a harbor was developed and land was chipped away for factories. The dunes weren't completely safe until 1971, when the state government created the Dunes Nature Preserve.

One woman, the writer Juliet Strauss, led the battle to save the forest at Turkey Run. Strauss learned in late 1915 that a timber company had bought the vast forest near her Rockville home and planned to cut down the trees. "Who would have dreamed a few men's dollars could step in and destroy . . . the most beautiful spot in Indiana," she said.

Strauss dashed off a letter to Indiana governor Samuel Ralston. Within a week, Ralston appointed Strauss to a committee to save the forest. Strauss wrote biting articles about "timber wolves" in her regular *Indianapolis News* column, "The Country Contributor." Her persistence inspired the community to collect $40,000 to buy the land from the timber firm. Strauss is honored with a statue and a display of her achievements at Turkey Run State Park.

More recently, local lawmakers created programs to protect the air, water, and land. In 1995 alone, Indiana residents threw away 5.8 million tons of garbage. That's equal to the weight of 725,000 adult elephants! Like other states, Indiana is running out of places to dump its garbage. Legislators passed laws that would cut the amount of waste in half by the year 2001. The plan called for statewide programs to teach the public to "reduce and recycle" waste and to compost yard debris. Nine hundred government workers were hired to measure pollution and to develop teaching and recycling programs statewide.

"What we do for the environment is education through tours and park exhibits," says Randy Reed, a Turkey Run park ranger. "We show people a tiny piece of what Indiana looked like before people came."

Wolf Park, in West Lafayette, created Howl Night to remind

people to protect the environment for animals. Every Friday, visitors can see packs of wolves mingle with bison in seminatural park settings. At 7:30 P.M., onlookers howl at the wolves.

Local corporations have pitched in by accepting recycled items. They have studied ways to use the throwaways in products they sell. Cities like Muncie require the recycling of paper and metals that can be sold as raw materials for new goods.

Groups of concerned Indiana citizens continue to watch over their environment. From Yellowwood State Forest to the Calumet region, people question factory growth, logging, and road and building development. They are working hard to preserve the natural beauty of their state.

A trip to the Indiana Dunes is a fun way to learn about the environment.

2 ALL-GOLDEN YESTERDAYS

Oaks of Vernon by Brown County painter Theodore Steele

T.C.Steele .87

I catch my breath as children do
In woodland swings when life is new . . .
When buds of Spring begin to blow
In blossoms that we used to know,
And lure us back along the ways
Of time's all-golden yesterdays!
James Whitcomb Riley, "The All Golden"

James Whitcomb Riley was Indiana's most popular poet in the early 1900s. His poems evoke a state free of big-city differences, a place where people embrace similar ideas. His "people's poetry" describes neighbors who are friendly and proud and share a common past. Yet Riley overlooked much of what makes Indiana history so exciting—the joys and clashes of its many different voices.

EARLY SETTLEMENT

The first people who roamed the region, about ten thousand years ago, were hunters. They followed waterways in search of bison, elk, and deer. These early wanderers left no written records. But archaeologists have uncovered animal and human bones, shells, and stone tools—clues to the simple roving life these people lived.

The prehistoric people who followed settled along the riverbeds.

From 1000 B.C. to about A.D. 1500 they developed small farm communities, growing squash, pumpkins, and other seed plants. They carved stone tools, molded clay pots, and carried mud from the riverbeds to build large earth mounds for their dead. Historians have named these people "mound builders."

Later mound builders learned to plant corn and hunt with bows and arrows. Their flat-topped mounds were grand ceremonial centers in addition to burial grounds. Mounds, many of which can still be seen today, were scattered over much of Indiana.

"At Angel Mounds, we have one of the best-preserved ancient Indian settlements in the United States," says Rodney Richardson of Angel Mounds.

Angel Mounds has eleven earthworks along the Ohio River. The tallest of these forms three terraces and is 44 feet high. Its 644-

A visit to Angel Mounds near Evansville is a journey into the distant past. The fate of the people who built these wondrous earthworks continues to baffle historians today.

foot-long stockade wall is the largest prehistoric structure in the eastern United States.

Historians believe Angel Mounds served as a capital for many smaller settlements nearby. At its peak, about three thousand people lived in the village. By 1450, however, the settlement was empty. Some scientists think the inhabitants ran out of food and died. Others believe they disbanded and became the ancestors of later Native American nations.

MOVING WEST

Smaller groups of corn farmers dotted Indiana country for the next two hundred years. Then waves of Miami, Potawatomi, and Kick-apoo migrated southward from the Great Lakes region. European settlers from the colonies forced the Delaware, Munsee, and Shawnee from their homelands in the East.

French fur trader René-Robert Cavelier, sieur de La Salle was the first known European to scout Indiana. In 1679 he reached the "south bend" of the Saint Joseph River, where present-day South Bend lies. "Those lands surpass all others in everything," he wrote eagerly to the king of France.

The following year La Salle returned to explore northern Indiana. Other French fur traders brought blankets, whiskey, and jewels to swap for skins. Trappers, missionaries, and explorers followed. By 1732 the French had built three trading posts along the Wabash River: Fort Ouiatenon (near present-day Lafayette), Fort Miami (now Fort Wayne), and Vincennes. They hoped to secure Native American trade routes from Lake Erie to the Mississippi River.

In Ezra Winter's mural, Vincennes: The British Barrier to the West, *colonists under George Rogers Clark attack the British at Fort Sackville. Of this victory, Clark said, "Great things have been effected by a few men well conducted."*

The British competed with the French to control the fur trade. Fighting between the two countries broke out during the 1750s. Many Indian tribes sided with France in what was called the French and Indian War. By the time the battles ended in 1763, France had lost all land west of the colonies.

Native Americans refused to admit defeat, however. Ottawa chief Pontiac gathered the Seneca, Ojibwa, Potawatomi, and other neighboring tribes to drive the British from the Great Lakes region. Pontiac's forces swept through Fort Ouiatenon and destroyed Fort Miami. Soldiers finally stopped them at Fort Detroit, at least for a while.

In 1775 another war erupted. This time the colonists fought to free themselves from British rule. Most fighting during the Revolutionary War took place in the East. But George Rogers Clark, who had moved from Virginia, pleaded for an army to help settlers fight the British in the west. "If a country is not worth protecting," he argued, "it is not worth claiming."

Clark's army won two major battles at Vincennes. The troops cut off British soldiers attacking colonists from the west. Clark's successes helped change the course of the war. Soon after, the colonists were free to form an independent nation.

FROM TERRITORY TO STATE

Present-day Indiana, Illinois, Ohio, Wisconsin, Michigan, and part of Minnesota became the Northwest Territory in 1787. Stories spread about the fertile, unpopulated region to the west. Wagon trains of pioneers who were tired of crowded towns in the eastern states set out to seek their fortunes. Settlers from Virginia and Kentucky paddled boats along the Ohio River.

"The emigrants who settled in Indiana at an early date came over the trails made by the Indians," wrote Colonel William Cockrun in 1907. "[They found] nothing but what they could manufacture and devise. . . . They had the great book of nature before them and were happy studying its changing scenes."

This flood of settlers horrified the Native Americans. The Miami, Shawnee, Wea, and Delaware formed raiding parties to scare invaders off the land. Miami chief Little Turtle led the most crushing blows against troops in the Wabash Valley.

The army was called to protect the settlers. General Anthony Wayne's soldiers struck back at the Battle of Fallen Timbers on August 20, 1794. Wayne and his troops surrounded Little Turtle's army along the Maumee River, near present-day Toledo, Ohio, and kept charging until the Indians fled into the woods.

After the battle, Wayne's troops headed north along the river. They plundered Indian crops and villages until they reached the place where the Saint Mary and Saint Joseph Rivers meet in Indiana. Here, Wayne built a fort and named it after himself.

Little Turtle and his people were heartsick at the sweeping ruin Wayne had left behind. "The Americans are now led by a chief who never sleeps," Little Turtle said of his enemy.

New troops arrived to guard the forts. Indian raids stopped for the next fifteen years. When Ohio gained statehood in 1800, the remaining land in the Northwest Territory became the Indiana Territory.

President Thomas Jefferson chose William Henry Harrison as territory governor and Vincennes as the headquarters. Jefferson ordered Harrison to protect settlers from unfriendly Indians. Harrison decided to silence the Indians by buying their land along the Ohio River and forcing them to move.

"Sell a country?" raged Shawnee chief Tecumseh. "Why not sell the air, the clouds, and the great sea as well as the earth?"

In 1810, Tecumseh resolved to unite territory tribes. He and his brother Tenskwautawa, the Prophet, gave fiery speeches against the sale of land to European settlers. Tecumseh charged that Indiana lands were "common property of the tribes and no one tribe had the right to cede land without consent of all."

Tecumseh's outraged supporters formed Prophetstown, a village along the Tippecanoe River. Harrison countered by raising an army and building Fort Harrison nearby, which became a target for attacks from Prophetstown.

Tecumseh's death at the 1813 Battle of the Thames, pictured by Nathaniel Currier, left the band of tribes without a strong leader.

Harrison used the attacks as an excuse to invade the village. Only he waited until Tecumseh was away. On a rainy November 7, 1811, Harrison's forces and the Prophet's followers clashed in the night. Each suffered heavy losses at the Battle of Tippecanoe. By daylight the Prophet ordered his people to flee as Harrison destroyed their village. (Thirty years later, Harrison would become the nation's ninth president. His campaign slogan harked back to his days as an Indian fighter: "Tippecanoe and Tyler [his vice president] Too.")

After the attack, Tecumseh rushed from tribe to tribe rallying warriors. For almost two years, his followers killed and kidnapped settlers and burned their homes. In September 1813, Tecumseh was killed in the Battle of the Thames.

Without their forceful leader, the Indians no longer attacked. Some Native Americans fled to Ohio and Detroit and were later forced west. Others retreated to their villages. Although settlers and Indians clashed from time to time, Native Americans had pretty much lost control of the Wabash. A new era of settlement had begun.

Thirty years after William Henry Harrison's forces crushed Tecumseh's people in the Battle of Tippecanoe, Harrison became President of the United States.

TIP AND TY

This song was written for the 1840 presidential campaign in which William Henry Harrison ran against Martin Van Buren. Harrison had been governor of Indiana when he led a victory over the Indians at the Tippecanoe River (near present-day Lafayette) in 1811. By 1840, he was known as "Old Tippecanoe" or simply "Tip."

Harrison won the election but died after only one month in office. Vice President John Tyler, known as "Ty," succeeded him.

Van.   Van is a used - up man, And with them we'll beat lit - tle Van.

Like the rushing of mighty waters,
    waters, waters,
On it will go!
And in its course will clear the way
For Tippecanoe and Tyler too. *Chorus*

See the Loco standard tottering,
    tottering, tottering,
Down it must go!
And in its place we'll rear the flag
Of Tippecanoe and Tyler too. *Chorus*

Let them talk about hard cider, cider,
    cider,
And Log Cabins too,
It will only help to speed the ball
For Tippecanoe and Tyler too. *Chorus*

Don't you hear from every quarter,
    quarter, quarter,
Good news and true?
That swift the ball is rolling on
For Tippecanoe and Tyler too. *Chorus*

The Bay State boys turned out in
    thousands, thousands, thousands,
Not long ago,
And at Bunker Hill they set their seals
For Tippecanoe and Tyler too. *Chorus*

Have you heard from old Vermount,
    mount, mount,
All honest and true?
The Green Mountain boys are rolling the ball
For Tippecanoe and Tyler too. *Chorus*

His latchstring hangs outside the door,
    door, door,
And is never pulled through,
For it never was the custom of
Old Tippecanoe and Tyler too. *Chorus*

He always has his tables set, set, set,
For all honest and true,
To ask you in to take a bite
With Tippecanoe and Tyler too. *Chorus*

Little Matty's days are numbered, numbered, numbered,
Out he must go!
And in his place we'll put the good
Old Tippecanoe and Tyler too. *Chorus*

KIE-BOON-MIEN-KA ("WE QUIT PICKING") POWWOW

In 1996, 15,200 Indiana residents claimed Native American ancestry. These numbers represent 105 different tribes. To celebrate their heritage, Native Americans hold several ceremonies, or powwows, around the state.

Every September in South Bend, the Pokagon band of Potawatomi run the largest Indiana powwow. About twelve thousand people attend Kie-boon-mien-ka, meaning "We Quit Picking," to mark the end of huckleberry-picking season. The ceremony begins with a grand entry at high noon, when the power of the sun, the creator, is greatest. A flag song follows, honoring U.S. and Canadian flags and the Eagle Staff, the pole with eagle feathers that represents warriors of old. A veteran's song honoring those who served in United States wars and a friendship dance call everyone together. The rest of the day is for dancing, displaying native beadwork and pottery, and feasting on fried bread, grape dumplings, and buffalo burgers.

A STATE COMES ALIVE

Before Fort Harrison was built, fewer than one thousand European settlers were scattered through Indiana Territory. By 1813 almost 64,000 settlers had made their homes in the Ohio Valley. Wagonloads of settlers were streaming in. Territorial government moved to a more central location, in Corydon.

Thomas Lincoln migrated with his family to southwest Indiana in 1816. He raised his famous son, Abraham, from age seven to twenty-one in Spencer County before relocating the family to Illinois. Abraham didn't think much of his log-cabin schooling in Indiana. "There was absolutely nothing to excite ambition for education," he recalled as president.

Indiana, meaning "Indian land," became the nineteenth state on December 11, 1816. As the state's population grew, so too did the need for more industry and, of course, land. Native Americans occupied the state's rustic northern two-thirds. The first elected governor, Jonathan Jennings, pressured the chiefs to sell land in middle Indiana. Afterward, he sent commissioners to lay out a village in the heart of the state. In 1824 the state capital was moved from Corydon to Indianapolis, its present site.

"The state treasurer moved state records in four oxcarts. The 125-mile trip took ten days," read Corydon records.

Without the threat from Native Americans, the state's population exploded to almost 150,000 people. British and Scots-Irish pioneers from the south and east farmed and traded goods in central Indiana towns. Scandinavians farmed the eastern border, and German immigrants headed for the south. The *Indiana Gazette*,

Indiana pioneers had to clear acres of first-growth forest before they could begin to farm.

the state's first newspaper, attracted newcomers by printing, "No soil produces a greater abundance than that of Indiana."

CROSSROADS OF AMERICA

For the next twenty years, towns expanded near main water and land routes. Irish workers arrived to build canals and roads. Construction of the Wabash and Erie Canal in Wabash County opened the river to flatboat and steamboat traffic from the Great Lakes.

The *Florence*, the first steamboat to visit Terre Haute, arrived in about 1823. Fifteen years later, eight hundred steamers hauled grain, pork, and whiskey from bustling Indiana cities. The boats returned with more immigrants, attracted to land that sold for $1.25 an acre.

Indiana's stretches of the east-west National Road (now U.S. 40) and the north-south Michigan Road (now U.S. 421, Indiana routes 29 and 25, and U.S. 31) opened during the 1830s. These routes created direct overland links between the East and the West. Twelve stagecoach lines carted passengers through Indianapolis along the National Road. Many new roads connected the highways to smaller Indiana towns. Mines, quarries, mills, and factories sprang up near these routes.

"Most roads were only mud with deep ruts, water holes, and occasional rocks and boulders which made travel slow and difficult," remembers Otis Buckley of Geneva.

In 1847 the first major Indiana railroad linked Madison and Indianapolis. Within three years, railroad tracks in Indiana increased tenfold, making steamboats outdated. Most cross-country railroad lines passed through Indiana, as did highways, earning Indiana its motto, "Crossroads of America."

Sometime in the mid-1800s, Indiana residents adopted the nickname Hoosiers. Many claim the word comes from the pioneer custom of greeting callers with "Who's yere?" One story links the name to workers of the canal builder Samuel Hoosier. Another legend traces *Hoosier* to the word *husher*, meaning "a strong riverboat worker," or to *hoozer*, a slang word for "hill dweller." Whatever the origin, the name stuck.

CIVIL WAR

Slavery was banned in Indiana at statehood. By 1850, 405 African Americans lived in Indianapolis. Yet the state was split over the issue of slavery.

Many European settlers had come from Southern states, where it was common to own slaves. These people tended to accept the cruel practice. Other Hoosiers actively opposed slavery. A heavily trafficked portion of the Underground Railroad (the hideaways along the path to freedom) ran through eastern Indiana. Antislavery Quakers Levi and Katherine Coffin operated an important stop along the route in Fountain City.

If runaways and those who helped them were captured, the punishments—beatings, jail, even death—were harsh. The Coffins dug an indoor well to hide the amount of water they used from outsiders. Many owners tracked their slaves to the house, only to find the footprints had disappeared.

"There must be an Underground Railroad and Levi Coffin must be the president and his house the Grand Central Station," cried the angry owners. During their twenty years in Fountain City, Levi and Katherine Coffin helped two thousand runaways reach safety.

The Civil War, between the North and the South, broke out in 1861. As a Northern state, Hoosiers fought on the side of the Union to keep the country united. Some Hoosiers resented this. Still, nearly 210,000 men enlisted in the Union army, a larger number than from any other state besides New York. Only one battle was fought in Indiana; four guards were killed. Overall, more than 24,000 Hoosiers died in service—the greatest loss in Indiana military history.

An Indiana youth stands at attention in his brand new Union uniform. In their eagerness to fight in the Civil War, many teenagers lied about their age.

BOOM TIMES

Large numbers of African Americans migrated north after the Civil War. The strong-willed black minister John Clay worked tirelessly to bring his people from the South. "In Indiana all stand equal before the law. . . . hitch up your teams and come overland," pleaded Clay, himself a former runaway slave.

By 1880, blacks totaled 15,931, or 9 percent, of the Indianapolis population, more than in other Indiana towns and most northern cities. But skilled jobs and many neighborhoods were still closed to blacks. That same year, however, James Hinton became the first

African American elected to the state house of representatives.

Rapid industrial growth followed the war. Plenty of coal, natural gas, stone, oil, and trees attracted varied industries to the state. The east-central region earned the name "gas belt" for its seemingly endless supply of natural gas. Glassmaking, which needed large amounts of gas, grew into a major industry in the state. With 110 plants, Indiana developed into the second-largest glass producer in the nation. Muncie became known as "Glass Town" for the Ball Corporation, a leading jar manufacturer that thrives today.

Other industries led to the growth of towns. Bedford was called the "limestone capital of America" for its rich supply of quality building rock. Sarah Breedlove (Madam C. J.) Walker and Colonel Eli Lilly each employed hundreds of workers in their Indianapolis plants. Walker's hair-care products for African-American women made her the nations's first black millionaire. By developing insulin, which controls life-threatening diabetes, Lilly's researchers saved countless lives.

During the late 1800s, Hoosiers revolutionized transportation equipment. In 1894, Elwood Haynes of Kokomo built the first gas-run automobile. Haynes recalled that during the test drive, his invention "moved off at a speed of about seven miles per hour and was driven about one and a half miles farther . . . without making a single stop." Observers called the machines that Haynes manufactured "horseless carriages."

The Studebaker brothers owned the country's largest horse-drawn wagon factory, in South Bend. Within ten years, they had converted the company into a booming car industry. Major factory towns appeared in northern Indiana to support the expanding

THE WALKER METHOD FOR SUCCESS

Madam C. J. Walker, born Sarah Breedlove, was once a washer-woman in Vicksburg, Mississippi. After moving to Saint Louis, Missouri, she created a cream that made tight, curly hair easier to style. At first she mixed the oils and soaps in a washtub and sold the cream door-to-door.

Walker was so successful that in 1910 she built a factory in Indianapolis to manufacture products. By then, her Walker Method included shampoo, hair-growth pomade, vigorous brushing, and application with a heated metal comb. Walker also established a training center for her growing sales staff, the hallmark of her success. Walker offered inexperienced black women better pay and working conditions and, best of all, a job with dignity.

"I have made it possible for many colored women to abandon the washtub," she would say.

business. Oil refineries and steel mills transformed the small villages of Whiting, Hammond, Gary, and East Chicago, places once known for their white pines and huckleberries. Automobile-related industries continued to expand throughout the state well into the twentieth century.

SMOKESTACKS AND CORNFIELDS

Improved and expanded industry hurt Indiana farmers, though. Northern swamps around factory towns were turned into farmland, glutting the market with more crops. Expensive steam-powered plows and threshers boosted production even more. As a result, crop prices fell, while the cost of harvesting increased. By 1900, 30 percent of Hoosier farmers were forced to sell their land and move to cities for better-paying jobs. For the first time, more Hoosiers earned their living in factories than on farms.

Factory workers often withstood terrible living and working conditions. Many toiled twelve hours a day six days a week for as little as fifteen cents an hour. Eugene Debs of Terre Haute achieved national acclaim as a "friend of the worker." Debs believed

When Elwood Haynes sputtered down the road in his gas-powered buggy, some people stopped to stare, while others scattered like frightened chickens.

workers could change unfair labor practices by joining together in unions, such as the American Railway Union he organized during the 1890s.

Debs also argued for women's and children's rights. But his unpopular stands against factory owners and against Americans fighting in World War I landed him in jail. Refusing to give up, Debs took his pleas for fair treatment to the people. He ran for president five times as the candidate of the Socialist Party, including once from jail in 1920. That year he received almost a million votes!

"While there is a lower class I am in it," he declared. "While there is a soul in prison I am not free."

RISE AND FALL OF THE KLAN

Waves of African Americans from the South took jobs in the expanding steel mills and factories of Evansville, South Bend, and Gary. Thousands of immigrants from Poland, Hungary, Lithuania, Italy, and Mexico filled neighborhoods in the thriving towns of the Calumet region. Many longtime residents believed that the newcomers were a threat to their well-being.

"Often bias in Indiana as elsewhere resulted from the fear of losing jobs," wrote historian John Bodnar.

During the 1920s, Indiana became a stronghold of a national hate group, the Ku Klux Klan (KKK). White-hooded members of the Klan beat and bullied Catholics, Jews, and, especially, African Americans. The racist organization became so widespread that it sponsored women's clubs, children's contests, parades, and family outings. Individuals who opposed the Klan's ideas and

In the early twentieth century, Gary children celebrate their many ethnic heritages at the public library.

its use of violence risked their businesses and lives and those of family members.

In Indiana the Klan's most powerful leader was David Curtis Stephenson. Everyone in the state—the governor, mayors, judges, and local school boards—took orders from this Grand Dragon of hate. "I am the law and power in Indiana," warned Stephenson.

THE SPIRIT OF HOOSIERLAND

During World Wars I and II, Indiana ranked seventh in state output of war goods. Gunpowder, food for troops, and trucks went overseas. Existing factories were enlarged and new plants were built to manufacture military products, attracting thousands of workers to the state.

Studebaker produced trucks that were sent to the Soviet Union.

POPULATION GROWTH: 1810–1990

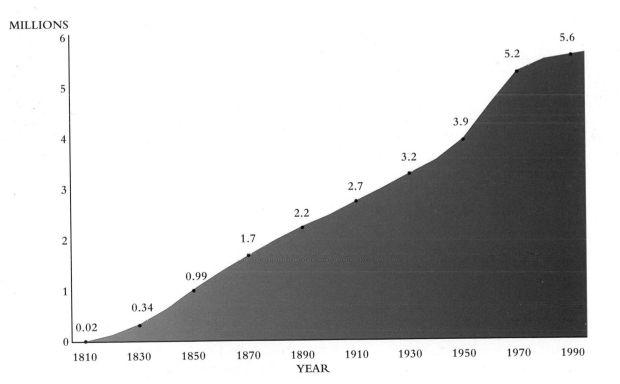

So many vehicles displayed the company name that Soviet soldiers thought *Studebaker* was English for *truck.*

The decades following World War II were periods of rapid growth in Indiana. As in the rest of the nation, its cities were bursting at the seams. Suburbs overflowed onto flat farmland. Interstate highways drew shoppers to malls away from downtown areas. By the 1960s, giant corporations began to close, too, leaving cities with high unemployment and decaying downtowns.

As a result, race riots erupted in many troubled cities around the country. Indiana towns, however, rarely faced this threat of

Easy living is a quality that lingers in small-town Indiana.

racial violence. In 1967, Gary voters elected Richard Hatcher as mayor, the first black head of a major city in the United States.

Still, serious differences persisted in income and housing between black and white Hoosiers. To close the gap between rich and poor, many towns began programs to turn the economy around for all Hoosiers. The late 1980s and early 1990s were periods of renewal in which the state sought to enliven city centers and attract new industries. Historic landmarks received face-lifts. Large cities, like Indianapolis, built stadiums, museums, and parks to draw Hoosiers and out-of-staters alike.

Most improvements come slowly. Downtown Indianapolis and Terre Haute bustle with new construction. In towns like Kentland and New Middleton, however, empty factories and run-down homes remain as ghostly reminders of the businesses that have gone.

In spite of many changes, Indiana cities have kept their small-town feeling. Hoosiers retain the ability to relax even in the midst of economic downturns or fast-paced city life. As Irving Liebowitz wrote in *My Indiana*:

Generally speaking, Hoosiers have learned the value of the simple things in life. They are in no great rush and are not overawed by wealth, position or prestige. Hoosiers may live in the present and plan for the future, but they jealously guard the past.

3 RUNNING HOOSIERLAND

The capitol in Indianapolis

"Yes, the old state . . . has struck a right good average," said Indiana-born vice president Thomas Marshall in 1913. "It has surely furnished as many first-grade second-class men in every department of life as any state in the Union."

During the 1920s, Robert and Helen Merrell Lynd studied Muncie, Indiana, as a "typical American community." They published reports in 1929 and 1937 hailing Muncie as Middletown, a place where average Americans were sensible and independent. Soon all Hoosiers were said to display these "down-home" traits in the way they governed, worked, and learned.

INSIDE GOVERNMENT

Hoosiers manage the most productive state government in the Midwest. Indiana receives the fewest federal dollars of all fifty states. Yet the state has low taxes, little debt, and a smaller public workforce than any other state in the Midwest. The trade-off is that citizens receive fewer public services, such as sick pay and public housing. Parents even have to rent their children's textbooks.

Indiana government is divided into three separate departments: executive, legislative, and judicial. As in the federal government, the

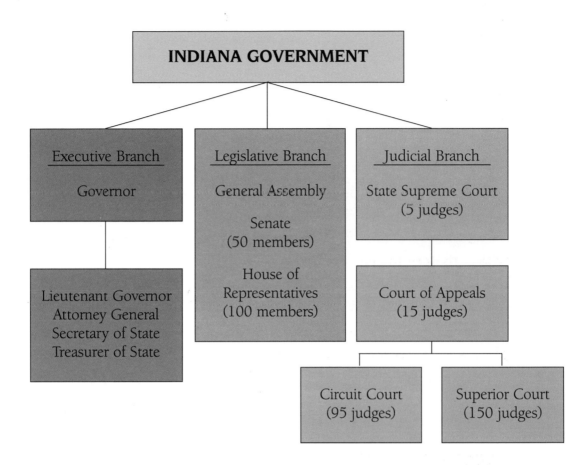

INDIANA GOVERNMENT

Executive Branch

Governor

Lieutenant Governor
Attorney General
Secretary of State
Treasurer of State

Legislative Branch

General Assembly

Senate
(50 members)

House of
Representatives
(100 members)

Judicial Branch

State Supreme Court
(5 judges)

Court of Appeals
(15 judges)

Circuit Court
(95 judges)

Superior Court
(150 judges)

departments check one another in making, interpreting, or carrying out the laws.

Executive. The state's chief executive officer is the governor. Every four years, Hoosiers choose a governor, who appoints state workers, signs or vetoes (rejects) bills, commands the state military, and oversees seven elected officers who run various state agencies.

In 1988, Evan Bayh won the Democratic Party its first governor's office in twenty-four years. Bayh was only thirty-two years old, young for such an important position. Four years later, voters

"My mother had a major influence on my life," said Evan Bayh in 1996. "Many people said that if she had lived in a different time, she would have been the United States senator."

reelected Bayh by the widest vote of any Hoosier governor in the twentieth century. He was especially popular with women voters, who were pleased to see more females heading important agencies during his administration than in most other states.

Legislative. Indiana's two-chamber legislature is called the general assembly. The fifty members in the senate are elected for four years. The one hundred members of the house of representatives serve for two-year terms. Hoosier legislators tend to stay in office for several terms, longer than in most other states. "We have the best legislature money can buy" is an old joke in the statehouse.

A key legislative job is to make laws. A majority of all members in each chamber must approve a bill before it can become law. Then the bill goes to the governor, who either signs the bill into law or vetoes it. Even if the governor rejects a bill, it can still become law if a majority in both houses overrides the veto. Indiana is unusual in requiring a majority of more than half the votes to override. Most other states require a two-thirds majority.

In 1972, Julia Carson became the first black woman to serve in the state house of representatives. She sponsored bills to benefit women and the poor, including a minimum-wage law for domestic workers. In 1976, Carson made history again, as the first black woman to be elected a state senator.

Judicial. The judicial department interprets laws and hears cases against individuals or businesses. A five-member supreme court and a fifteen-judge court of appeals are Indiana's highest courts. Ninety-five circuit courts and many county and special courts hear cases closer to home.

LOCAL LOYALTIES

Indiana, like many other states, has a jumble of smaller, overlapping government districts. The state has 92 counties, 1,008 townships, 115 cities, and 460 towns. Ideally, local agencies cooperate to run schools, police, and highway construction.

In 1970, Mayor Richard Lugar pushed through a program to combine the resources of Indianapolis city with those of the surrounding county. City and Marion County governments formed "Unigov," short for "unified government." The plan enlarged Indianapolis to Marion County borders and decreased government agencies from sixty to six.

Counties were a form of local government before statehood and before larger population centers developed. Hoosiers continue to think of themselves as coming from a county. Most residents give directions by county rather than by nearness to a city or a town. This can be confusing to a visitor who is unfamiliar with Indiana county names and borders.

Indiana government has a history of farmers battling the city folk. Because local loyalties are strong in Indiana, few Hoosiers have gained power beyond state borders. Only a small number of Hoosiers have earned national government acclaim. William Henry Harrison, Indiana territorial governor, became president of the United States in 1841. But he died thirty-one days after taking office. His grandson Benjamin Harrison, the only other Hoosier president, served from 1889 until 1893.

Being second in command seems to suit Hoosiers better. The United States has had five vice presidents from Indiana. Hoosiers call the state the "mother of vice presidents."

HOOSIERS AT WORK

"Indianapolis, like other Indiana towns, does not depend on one industry. It's diversified, so the city doesn't shut down if one industry folds," noted one resident.

Hoosiers have seen the problems of running single-business towns. When the steel industry declined in the 1980s, twenty-two thousand jobs were lost in Gary alone. Crime soared and unemployment skyrocketed as businesses left the city.

Therefore, towns—from Muncie and Terre Haute to Gary and Evansville—are seeking to produce a surprising variety of goods.

Indiana may be small in size among the states, but it remains in the top ten for factory and farm output.

Manufacturing. Indiana ranks an amazing second in the nation for manufactured goods. One in seven jobs is linked directly to goods exported from the country. Some industries, such as transportation equipment, containers, and steel, have remained national leaders since the early 1900s.

Fiery molten steel flows into holding tanks at Gary furnaces. U.S. Steel Gary Works produces almost eight million tons of raw steel a year.

The heart of Indiana manufacturing is still in the Calumet region, where steel is king. Even with major cutbacks, blast furnaces in Burns Harbor, East Chicago, and Gary remain the world's leading steel producers. Much of the steel goes into manufacturing transportation-related equipment.

Raw steel is shipped to factories throughout Indiana to produce parts for cars, trucks, and airplanes. Then parts are transported to assembly plants near Lafayette and Fort Wayne. More cargo trailers for trucks are produced by Lafayette's Wabash National Corporation than anywhere else in the United States.

Elkhart County, in northern Indiana, has been called the "recreational vehicle (RV) capital of the world." The trend began after the 1933 Chicago World's Fair, where Elkhart's Wilbur Schult saw a vehicle made by trailer pioneer Ray Gilkison of Terre Haute. Schult determined to produce a better trailer and eventually did, becoming an industry leader.

By the 1960s, three brothers from Elkhart had devised a way to

1992 GROSS STATE PRODUCT: $122 BILLION

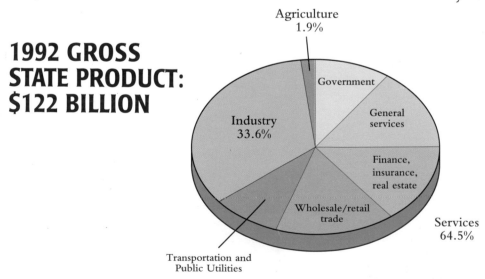

Agriculture
1.9%

Government

General services

Finance, insurance, real estate

Industry
33.6%

Wholesale/retail trade

Services
64.5%

Transportation and Public Utilities

EARNING A LIVING

Manufacturing

Chemicals

Electrical & electronic products

Food processing

Machinery

Steel

Transportation

Agriculture

Beef Cattle

Corn

Hogs

Soybeans

Tobacco

Vegetables

Wheat

Natural Resources

Coal

Forest products

L Limestone

Oil

Sand, gravel

Lake Michigan

Hammond • Gary

South Bend • • Elkhart

Kankakee R.

Tippecanoe R.

Fort Wayne •

Huntington •

Logansport

Wabash R.

West Lafayette • Lafayette

Kokomo •

Marion •

Mississinewa R.

Muncie •

Frankfort •

White R.

Anderson •

Crawfordsville •

Eel R.

Richmond •

Indianapolis

Wabash R.

Terre Haute •

Brookville Lake

Greensburg •

Bloomington •

Columbus •

Monroe Lake

White R.

Bedford •

Madison •

Ohio R.

Vincennes • • Shoals

New Albany •

Patoka Lake

Evansville •

Ohio R.

remodel trailers into comfortable yet affordable homes. They opened Coachmen Industries, selling twelve mobile homes the first year. Today the company employs more than three thousand people and builds twelve homes a day. Indiana produces almost 60 percent of all trailers and mobile homes in the United States. Over half of these come from Elkhart.

During the 1920s, Elkhart was the "band instrument capital of the world," too. Elkhart gained fame for its clarinets, trombones, and flutes. Companies like Selmer expanded to sell wind, percussion, and string instruments. Today other states produce competing products. But Elkhart remains a top player in the musical instrument field.

Agriculture. Farmland blankets about 70 percent of Hoosierland. Indiana's vast system of roads, railways, and waterways enables farmers to deliver crops easily to state, national, and international markets.

Corn and soybeans account for about half of Indiana's yearly farm income. Related corn products, such as popcorn and cerealine, make Hoosiers industry leaders. Cerealine, which comes from processing corn into cornstarch, was originally developed in Columbus in 1880. This ingredient, the basis of the first dry, flaked cereals other than rolled oats, started a new trend in breakfast food.

Other important Hoosier crops are hay, oats, potatoes, and apples. Winter wheat covers much of central Indiana during cold weather. New Albany's tobacco market sells several million pounds of leaves each season.

Indiana ranks fifth among states in hog and chicken farming. Regions around Lafayette and Vincennes are strongholds of

Farmers sort ears of corn into a crib bound for market.

the state's hog production. Hoosier chickens provide more eggs than any other state in the country besides California. And Colonel Harland Sanders, of Henryville, Indiana, created the hugely successful Kentucky Fried Chicken restaurant chain.

The recent national trend toward fewer but larger farms hit Indiana hard. From the mid-1980s until the 1990s, the number of farms dropped from 88,000 to 65,000. The average size rose

THE POPCORN KING

Hoosier Orville Redenbacher experimented for twenty-four years at Purdue University to find "perfect popcorn that popped light and fluffy." In 1965 he produced a special popcorn that expanded to twice the size of other varieties. His invention eventually made him famous throughout North America and Europe. He sold his company, though, before sales had really begun to take off.

Each September since 1979, thousands of people have gathered in Valparaiso to celebrate Redenbacher and local popcorn growers at the Popcorn Festival. The first festival and its twelve-foot-diameter popcorn ball made the *Guinness Book of Records*. Today visitors find popcorn teen dances, popcorn kernel races, a parade, and any number of popcorn treats, including popcorn lollipops.

Orville Redenbacher stands with the junior popcorn king and queen.

Pigs graze freely on Indiana Amish farms.

by fifty-four acres, while the price of calves fell. As a result, many farmers sold their land and found factory jobs in nearby towns.

Farming still lies at the heart of Indiana, though. For ten days every August, farm-related activities are celebrated at the Indiana State Fair. Farm goods, homemade crafts, and farm equipment highlight the celebration. Families enjoy pig races, ballooning, fiddling contests, and a carnival.

Children compete in contests for the best-cared-for pig or rabbit or for the most original vegetable decoration. During the year, local 4-H groups around the state prepare boys and girls for the contests. Once 4-H programs included only livestock and home-care projects. Now Indiana children can learn about photography, computers, model making, and sports. In Dubois County, the 4-H slogan is "Learn by Doing."

Service with a Smile. Service industries account for 65 percent of Indiana jobs. Government accounts for the largest share of these jobs. But Hoosier transportation companies also hire large numbers of employees. Two of the nation's twenty largest commercial carriers maintain headquarters in Indiana. About thirty railroads employ workers to help carry freight across the state.

Indiana tourism is a small but growing service industry. Sports events, like the Indianapolis 500, lure the largest numbers of visitors. Local tourism revolves around community festivals and attractions. Even the smallest towns attract visitors with celebrations of town history, hometown heroes, and local products.

MINERAL RESOURCES

Coal mining flourished along the Wabash and Ohio Rivers during the late 1800s. Much of central Indiana's coal deposits have been mined since then. Still, coal remains the state's chief mineral, mined mostly in the southwest.

Oil was plentiful near Geneva around the beginning of the twentieth century. According to Geneva resident Otis Buckley, "Black gold played a major role in how people made a living and small villages and towns developed." Today oil drills operate west of Evansville and northeast of Indianapolis. One of the nation's richest oil deposits is in Whiting. Nearby, factories in East Chicago, Hammond, and Gary turn oil into petroleum products.

Vast limestone deposits lie in Lawrence County. Stonecutters prefer Indiana limestone because it is easy to dig from the ground and carve. Stone blocks from southern Indiana quarries have been carted nationwide to build such landmarks as Chicago's Art Institute, New York's Empire State Building, and the Pentagon near Washington, D.C.

Workers from the "land of limestone" claim that stonework is in their blood. "When I was a boy, there were ordinary families and there were stone families," wrote Jack Kendall in the book *In Stone Country*. "I came from a stone family. . . . Every morning I'd sit down to breakfast and all the talk was stone, stone, stone."

More than 350,000 fans watch race cars whiz around the track at breakneck speeds during the Indianapolis 500.

4 DOWN-HOME HOOSIERS

"**Y**'*all* have a nice day," calls a Corydon Hoosier with a southern drawl. "I work in *de* region," explains one Calumet worker.

The way many Hoosiers talk is a clue to where they live in the state. Generally, the farther north in Indiana, the more *th* becomes *d* and a midwestern big-city twang appears. Central Hoosiers add an *r* to some words, saying *Worshington* instead of *Washington*. South of Bloomington, people have the southern drawl of their ancestors, who came from Kentucky or Virginia.

With sizable Mexican populations in the Calumet region, Koreans in Muncie, and Japanese in Lafayette, the state blends speech patterns from around the world. These are the many voices of Indiana. Add their folklore and traditions and you have the heart and soul of Hoosierland—its everyday people.

SMALL-TOWN FOLK

"Northwest Indiana is big enough to be interesting and little enough where everyone knows everyone else," says Indiana University student Katherine Belcher.

Indiana has about 5.5 million people and ranks fourteenth in population among the fifty states. Its population has hardly changed since 1980. Few Hoosiers leave, but fewer outsiders come to Indiana. With an average of 154 people per square mile, there

Farms and ranches surround Hoosier population centers.

is a livable blend of elbow room and neighbors.

"People are sick of huge cities," observes one Nashville resident. "My whole family moved to Brown County from San Diego, California."

Few Hoosier cities are bursting at the seams. Instead, the state contains about sixteen scattered population centers of at least thirty-five thousand people each. Most of these are county seats, complete with a fancy courthouse, war memorial, and local government buildings. About one-third of Hoosiers live in towns with fewer than two thousand people.

The largest city is the state capital, Indianapolis. Its metropolitan area includes 1,380,491 people, more than 20 percent of the state's population. Fort Wayne (173,072) and Evansville (126,272)

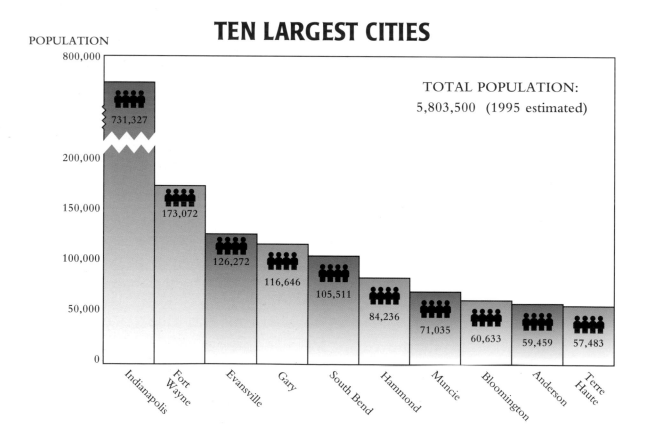

TEN LARGEST CITIES

POPULATION

TOTAL POPULATION:
5,803,500 (1995 estimated)

800,000

731,327

200,000

173,072

150,000

126,272

116,646

100,000

105,511

84,236

71,035

50,000

60,633

59,459

57,483

0

Indianapolis
Fort Wayne
Evansville
Gary
South Bend
Hammond
Muncie
Bloomington
Anderson
Terre Haute

are the state's next largest urban areas. Cities of the Calumet region, which are linked by the Calumet River, combine into a bustling population center.

WHO ARE HOOSIERS?

"People think of Indiana as a white bread state," explained Robert Taylor of the Indiana Historical Society. "We always had diversity. It just wasn't as obvious."

Only 10 percent of Indiana is nonwhite, mostly (8 percent) African American. Although less so than in some states, ethnic diversity has played a vital role in Indiana. The largest groups of residents remain of German, Scots-Irish, English, and French descent.

ETHNIC INDIANA

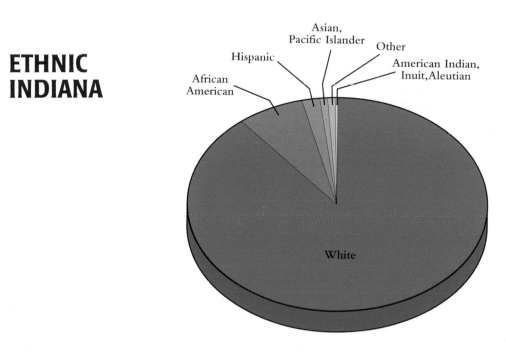

Pockets of Hoosiers still refuse to accept diversity. "Some people are blatant in racism," charges a Brown County resident. "I had a man spit in my face in the street because I was walking with a black friend."

Some southern Indiana towns have bad reputations among minorities. Small groups of Ku Klux Klan try to recruit members to their racist organization. A few times each year, they burn crosses on front lawns, a reminder of a time when the Klan controlled Indiana.

Larger numbers of Hoosiers work for racial understanding. The Indiana Humanities Council selects different cultures for communities to highlight. From 1996 to 1999, Hoosiers will explore their growing trade relationship with Asian countries. Asian fairs, videos, and lectures will give Hoosiers greater understanding of their neighbors from other lands.

Every fall, Columbus spotlights different cultures with a grand ethnic expo. Almost thirty-five thousand visitors enjoy three days of ethnic food booths, a street dance, an international bazaar, and art displays. A treat for the entire family is the kite fly.

"Kids make kites at the expo and fly them the next day at Clifty Park," says organizer Debra Lee. "We all fly together around the world."

DIFFERENT FAITHS

Religion in Indiana mirrors the state's ethnic mix. Roman Catholics maintain sizable Hoosier congregations. Smaller numbers of Indiana worshipers are members of the Protestant, Islamic, and Jewish

"We have 160 Japanese-owned companies in the state," said Steve Baker of the Indiana Humanities Council. "From 1996 to 1998 we will help communities organize exhibits, seminars, and festivals for 'Asia in Us,' the statewide program to learn more about [the] Pacific Rim countries of Japan, China, and Korea."

faiths. On the road west into Bloomington, a large Jewish center sits next to Baptist and Lutheran churches. So many churches and temples representing different beliefs line Hammond's Hohman Avenue that the street is known as "Church Row."

During the 1800s, several religious communities came to Indiana seeking a safe place to pray. Among the earliest groups were the Harmonists. In 1814, German religious leader George Rapp bought thirty thousand acres of southwest Indiana forest for his Harmonie Society. The peaceful Harmonists farmed, established mills and factories, and constructed 150 buildings. They named their successful town Harmony.

Social reformer Robert Owen and his financial partner William Maclure bought Harmony in 1825 and changed its name to New Harmony. Owen dreamed of a community that would "unite all interests into one." More than eight hundred scientists, scholars, and educators helped Owen create a learning center on the frontier.

The experiment in equality failed after three years. Still, Owen and Maclure pioneered many advances in equal rights and education, especially for women. Harmonist Fanny Wright boldly challenged current thinking that women were unequal to men, something women never dared to express in public. Her speeches were thought to be so shocking that men called women "Fanny Wrightists" as an insult.

Moravians founded the historic community of Hope in 1830 as part of the church's plan to expand along the frontier. The old Moravian Cemetery remains unchanged. Rows of limestone markers lie flat on the ground as a symbol of the Moravian belief that all people are equal in death.

Amish children take a break from farming, school, and household chores.

The Amish, a strict Mennonite sect, established farms outside Berne, in northeast Indiana, and in Daviess County. The Amish obey the Bible's warning to "be not conformed to this world." Members live very simply in farming communities. They forgo modern comforts like cars and electricity, dress in plain clothes, grow their own foods, and make tools and furniture by hand.

Men dress in mostly handmade, dark-colored hats and pants. Women wear long dark dresses and bonnets. Most Amish children ride to one-room schoolhouses in horse-drawn buggies. A visit through Amish country is a journey into an earlier time.

BOOK LEARNING

Hoosiers claim many firsts in education. In 1816, lawmakers wrote the first state constitution that required free public education. New Harmony thinkers introduced the nation to preschools, adult trade schools, and the idea of free public libraries. Harmonists offered some of the first public classes in which boys and girls studied together.

Even with these strong beginnings, Indiana was slow to provide equal education for all races. Black and white children would not go to the same schools for a long time. Usually, black schools received fewer funds and were poorly staffed. An exception was an African-American high school called Crispus Attucks, which opened in 1927. Attucks students traveled from the far corners of Indianapolis to attend classes. They were taught by an all-black faculty that drew from the best minds in the United States. Many talented black scholars taught high school instead of pursuing other careers because their skin color kept them from rising in their chosen fields.

"As a result, students received an excellent education from a stable staff," notes Gilbert Taylor, of the Crispus Attucks Center. "We have graduates in all walks of life now. Our alumni hold important jobs around the world in sizable numbers."

Indiana schools kept white and black students apart until a 1949 state law banned separate public education. Even then, segregation persisted in some areas for decades. Not until 1982 did statewide integrated education become a reality. To achieve racial balance, many of Attucks's more experienced teachers transferred to other schools. Now the school is an African-American learning center and museum within the Indianapolis school district. Gallery exhibits depict events in African-American history and house the state's high school basketball Hall of Fame.

Today, every Indiana child from age six to sixteen must attend school. As in many states, however, some districts turn out better-educated students than others. Overall, the state ranks a miserable forty-third in the nation on standardized tests and thirty-third in the number of high school dropouts. One in ten students enrolls in private school, partly to get a better education.

"We think our schools and teachers are very good," observes a

Students proudly pose before a display at the Crispus Attucks Center.

Noblesville teacher. "However, we find that kids who move here from other districts are always behind."

To improve education statewide, teachers developed ISTEP (Indiana Statewide Testing for Education Programs) in 1988. Hoosier students take ISTEP tests to learn which areas, if any, they need to improve. Another law, passed in 1995, attempts to reduce the number of students who drop out before high school graduation. Usually, Hoosier teens drive at age sixteen. But students who quit school early or skip too many classes must wait until their eighteenth birthday to apply for a driver's license.

Individual school districts, called corporations, plan many fun programs, too. Some districts join Young Authors, a program that gives budding writers the chance to shine. Often community businesses become involved with funding and displaying the final books in local shopping centers.

"We also encourage our students to support their communities," adds Marybeth Morgan, a state educator. "Students get into everything from adopting a flood-ravaged Illinois town to visiting senior citizens in a nursing home."

GETTING A COLLEGE EDUCATION

Hoosiers are proud of the state's more than forty public and private colleges and universities. The largest state-run institution, Indiana University, has eight campuses statewide. The main campus, with thirty thousand students, stretches for miles in Bloomington. Its many grand buildings house some of the finest university programs in the nation, particularly in music, law, and business. The univer-

Through the Sample Gates lies the main campus of Indiana University in Bloomington, among the most beautiful college campuses in the nation.

sity's Indianapolis campus runs the second-largest medical school in the country.

Purdue University's main campus, in Lafayette, excels in agricultural research, engineering, and, particularly, computer science. Another important area of research for the college is the aerospace industry.

Amelia Earhart, the first woman pilot to fly across the Atlantic Ocean, taught at Purdue. In 1929 she founded a group called the

Pilot Amelia Earhart (right) taught at Purdue, and astronaut Neil Armstrong (left) graduated from its aerospace school.

99s, whose members included 99 of the 117 women pilots in the country. Today the 99s is an international organization of about six thousand women. Purdue houses the largest collection of Earhart materials, including photos she took on her many flights and Coast Guard logs of the search to locate her lost plane.

Purdue's aerospace school has been nicknamed "mother of astronauts." Among its famous graduates is Mitchell-born Virgil Grissom, the first person to travel on two space flights. Neil Armstrong, another Purdue-trained astronaut, made the first walk on the moon. In 1984 alone, Purdue claimed seven astronauts trained for space travel.

Purdue has a mission to bring learning into communities. The university hires educators to work in every county of the state, presenting workshops about topics that affect Hoosiers. Educators form 4-H programs for boys and girls to develop leadership skills for the future. These teachers are even involved in planning the Indiana State Fair. As one Hoosier wrote, "The entire state has long been the Purdue University campus."

Surprisingly, Notre Dame, a private Catholic university known for its winning football team, has become a center for Mexican-American studies. Julian Samora had suffered many racial insults

During the mid-1990s, Hoosiers held festivals and programs to better understand their Mexican neighbors and trade partners.

FRIED BISCUITS

"Everything is fried in Indiana," says a shopkeeper, shaking her head.

Indiana is the land of biscuits and gravy, fried chicken, and country-fried steaks. Even the biscuits are fried here. Ask an adult to help you make this Hoosier recipe.

1/3 package dry yeast	1/4 cup vegetable oil
2 cups milk	2 teaspoons salt
1/8 cup sugar	3-1/2 to 4-1/2 cups flour

Add yeast to warm water according to packet directions. Add other ingredients and let dough stand until it puffs up, or rises. Pat dough and form into separate biscuits. Drop them into hot oil, which should cover the bottom of the frying pan. Fry on both sides until golden brown.

as a Mexican-American boy in southern Colorado. He vowed to combat prejudice with knowledge.

While a professor at Notre Dame, Samora helped found the National Council La Raza, a leading civil rights organization. He pioneered research on Mexican Americans in the Midwest. After Samora's death in 1996, Notre Dame created the Julian Samora Research Institute to expand his work on behalf of Mexican Americans.

HOOSIER KIDS LOVE HISTORY

Indiana has a rich network of history buffs. Some work for the library system, but many are volunteers. They publish and distribute information and support local historical societies and libraries. These include young historians, too.

In 1938, Indiana founded the Junior Historical Society, which is going strong today. Boys and girls from fourth grade through high school learn pioneer crafts, visit historic sites, and discover ways to preserve Indiana's past. Many go to summer history camp and the annual history convention. They learn about ancient digs and famous Hoosiers. Most of all, they learn that history can be fun.

Visitors watch craftspeople at the Covered Bridge Festival in Billie Creek Village, Rockville.

5 HOMETOWN HEROES

Fort Ouiatenon Historical Park

The winds of heaven never fanned
The circling sunlight never spanned
The borders of a better land
Than our own Indiana.

Sarah Bolton, Indianapolis

Hoosiers take great pride in their hometown heroes. Everyday Hoosiers eagerly trumpet their neighbors' accomplishments in the arts, architecture, and sports. They are especially proud that many folks who achieve national fame eventually return home to Indiana.

WRITERS AND COMICS

According to Indiana folklore, almost every Hoosier is a writer. As proof, humorist George Ade wrote a piece about a visiting author who invited writers from the audience to join him on stage. To his surprise, almost everybody rushed forward. The shocked speaker marveled that only one man, still seated, didn't think of himself as an author.

"He's just deaf and didn't hear what you said," someone replied. "He writes, too!"

In 1947, Purdue University librarian John Moriarity investigated whether Indiana really had more writers than other states. Moriarity happily discovered that Indiana ranked second only to

Children gather around their beloved poet, James Whitcomb Riley, and his dog.

New York State in the number of best-selling authors. (And New York had four times as many people!)

The early 1900s has been called the golden age of Indiana literature. Meredith Nicholson, George Ade, Gene Stratton Porter, and James Whitcomb Riley were some of the best-known authors. Nicholson once wrote that Indiana is "a state where not to be an author is to be distinguished."

Many Hoosiers described ideal country values for readers who felt trapped by dirty factories and crowded cities. Others wrote about nature. The author and naturalist Gene Stratton Porter adored Limberlost, the vast wooded swampland where she lived. She weaved her concern for the lush marsh into her novels *Freckles* and *A Girl of the Limberlost*. Stratton Porter moved from Limberlost in 1910, when the swamp was drained and the wildlife was gone. But she captured its splendor in photos and in more than twenty-three books, many that outsold the works of more acclaimed authors of the day.

James Whitcomb Riley described rural life in more than one thousand gentle poems. Boys and girls loved his poetry, earning Riley the title "children's poet." Riley's tender lines about an orphaned girl who had come to live with the Riley family as a servant touched a friend of his, Indianapolis cartoonist John Gruelle. He turned Riley's poem "Little Orphant Annie" into the character Raggedy Ann. Later, Riley's character inspired a Little Orphan Annie cartoon, play, and movie. Each year, during Riley Days Festival, the town of Greenfield holds a poetry reading of its hometown hero's rhymes.

Later Hoosier writers dealt with more serious issues of the day. Few people in Terre Haute thought much of young Theodore Dreiser, whom they called the "least employable" of the Dreisers. Probably that was because he dared to leave Indiana as a teenager. Dreiser returned long enough to write *A Hoosier Holiday*, while his songwriter brother, Paul, who had changed his name to Dresser, composed the state song. Still, Dreiser's nationally acclaimed novels *Sister Carrie* and *An American Tragedy* shocked Hoosiers with their terrible tales about industrial slums.

During World War II, reporter Ernie Pyle moved the nation with

Theodore Dreiser described Warsaw and other small towns where he lived in his 1916 book A Hoosier Holiday.

heart-wrenching stories about soldiers in battle. His articles ran nationwide, earning him a Pulitzer Prize for distinguished correspondence in 1944. No matter where Pyle traveled, however, his stories always seemed to turn homeward. "Indiana farmers know what the 'good neighbor' policy is," he wrote in *Home Country*. "It's born in them."

Today, another writer who grew up in Indiana, Kurt Vonnegut, continues to test Hoosier limits. Like Dreiser and Pyle, Vonnegut writes about human problems, not about the Hoosier ideal. Vonnegut mocks the Middle America that most Hoosiers stand for. He makes fun of foul-smelling factories, self-important adults, religion, and gun-toting hunters who claim to be peace loving. The

Ernie Pyle (center) listens to World War II reports over the ship loudspeaker three weeks before he was killed during the invasion of Okinawa, Japan.

Indianapolis-born author lives in the East now; most Hoosiers try to forget where he was raised.

Hoosier writers have always had a sense of humor. The most famous modern Hoosier cartoon character is Garfield the cat. Cartoonist Jim Davis has been drawing the lasagna-eating lazy beast in his Fairmount studio for more than ten years. Garfield reaches readers of 1,600 newspapers from twenty-two countries. The fun-loving cat has also been the subject of more than eleven best-selling books and two television specials, as well as the model

THE LEGEND OF PIKES PEAK

Indiana's Pikes Peak is named after the famous snow-capped Colorado rise in the Rocky Mountains even though there isn't a hill within half a mile of the Hoosier area. In *Home Country*, writer Ernie Pyle told how Brown County's Pikes Peak got its name. According to legend, a Brown County man got "western fever" in the mid-1800s. He sold his patch of land and all his furniture and loaded his wagon with several months' worth of supplies. Then he started west with PIKES PEAK OR BUST painted on the side of his wagon.

After a couple of weeks, the man grew terribly homesick. He returned home but had nothing left except a wagonload of supplies. To raise money, he pitched a tent and sold his supplies from the wagon. Bargain hunters were told to buy them from "that Pikes Peak feller." Brown County residents who came later kept the name.

for some five thousand Garfield items. Even with all the success, Garfield is as independent and stubborn as any real-life Hoosier. "Home," says Garfield, "is where they understand you."

CAPTURING INDIANA ON CANVAS

Indiana's countryside has inspired countless artists. In the early 1800s, craftspeople were drawn to New Harmony's School of Industry. Here budding artists learned drawing, weaving, sculpting, painting, and printing.

Art colonies soon developed around the state. By the early 1900s, the largest colony was in Brown County. Members devoted themselves to capturing the area's rugged beauty on canvas.

T. C. Steele painted at Bear Wallow in the wild Brown County hills.

Forested hills in autumn, log cabins, and scores of woodland creatures sparked wonderful images. These landscape painters became known as the Hoosier Group.

Artist Theodore Clement (T. C.) Steele loved Brown County so much that he built an eleven-room home and several art studios on 211 acres in the heart of its rolling hills and forests. His thriving community attracted painters, photographers, and, later, gallery owners and tourists. The community became one of the nation's most celebrated artists' colonies.

Today the Brown County art colony displays landscapes by Glen Cooper Henshaw and portraits by Marie Goth. Both artists painted in Steele's original art colony. A host of other landscape artists, potters, quilters, and weavers carry on the Hoosier Group tradition.

TOE TAPPERS

Every kind of music can be found in Hoosierland—jazz, rock, country, classical, and dance. The hub of the state's artistic activities, however, has been in Indianapolis. The city's symphony, opera company, jazz clubs, and theater draw Hoosiers from miles around.

During the 1920s, jazz wailed from clubs along the capital's Indiana Avenue, home of Madam C. J. Walker's theater and College of Beauty Culture. The street earned the name "Black Broadway" for its wealth of black entertainers and businesses. Jazz guitarist Wes Montgomery first strummed his "Indy Sound" on the "Grand Ol' Street." Guitarist Reginald DuValle popularized a form of jazz called ragtime in the Midwest. Today modern jazz and bebop blare from Hoosiers J. J. Johnson and Slide Hampton, two of the few jazz trombonists in the country.

Jazz greats influenced 1950s songwriter Hoagy Carmichael.

Songwriter Hoagy Carmichael dashed off many of his hit tunes in a single day.

He played his "hot piano" at Indiana University before leading his own band. Carmichael is best known for composing the classic "Stardust," as well as hundreds of other songs. He won a 1951 Academy Award for "In the Cool, Cool, Cool of the Evening."

Twyla Tharp uses jazz as one avenue for creating dances. She was born in Portland, Indiana, but her striking choreography is known throughout the nation. Tharp's dances blend ballet, modern, and tap dancing set to music that may move from classical or jazz to rock. Tharp has developed numbers for television programs, theater, and ice shows, and for her own dance company.

What really makes Hoosiers tap their feet is country and bluegrass music. The Indiana Fiddler's Gathering at Tippecanoe Battlefield State Memorial is an annual jam session of dulcimers, guitars, and mandolins playing southern hill tunes. At the state fair, country music is king.

Nashville, Indiana, even has its own Little Opry, named after the Grand Ole Opry in Nashville, Tennessee. Two thousand people crowd onto long rows of wooden benches to hear the finest country sounds this side of Tennessee. Country singer Julie Mainard and harmonica player Ronnie Murphy got their start in the Little Opry.

Bean Blossom locals say songwriter and mandolin player Bill Monroe practically invented bluegrass. His annual bluegrass festivals have drawn huge crowds since the mid-1960s. In 1992 the nationally recognized father of bluegrass built a Bluegrass Hall of Fame in Bean Blossom to exhibit his country and bluegrass souvenirs.

In 1871 Fort Wayne hosted the nation's first professional baseball game between the Kekiongas and Cleveland Forest Citys. It is only fitting that Hoosier Albert von Tilzer wrote the popular song "Take Me Out to the Ball Game." Von Tilzer, whose real name was Harry Gumbinsky, composed three thousand songs from his home on Indianapolis's South Side.

With the popularity of Indiana sports comes a strong interest in high school bands. Any town with a band contest winner puts up a street sign proclaiming the victory. The town of Brazil's sign reads BIG TEN STATE CHAMPS OF MARCHING BAND.

Indiana teenagers love their rock stars. Gary-born Janet and Michael Jackson stand out with top-selling CDs and videotapes. Lafayette's Axl Rose of Guns and Roses thrills audiences nation-wide. Seymour has given the music world hard-rock musician John Cougar Mellencamp. Today the famous rocker paints portraits at home in Bloomington. He is another Hoosier who left but couldn't stay away.

Singer Michael Jackson gives his sister Janet a kiss after she presented him with the 1993 Grammy Living Legend Award.

CELEBRITIES

Hoosiers claim many great performers. Indianapolis-born journalist Jane Pauley has hosted several television shows. She was one of the early women talk-show hosts during the 1970s, with such successes as the *Today Show* and, later, *Dateline NBC*.

James Dean, the celebrated actor, came from Fairmount. He died in 1955 in a car crash at the peak of his career. Still, Hoosiers—and middle-agers everywhere—worship the 1950s teen heartthrob. Dean's good looks and tough-guy acting style were special for the era. His movies *East of Eden* and *Giant* earned him Academy Award nominations after his death. Fairmount honors the local hero with museum exhibits and film displays at the annual Fairmount Museum Days Festival.

David Letterman once reported having been a C student at Ball State University. Now the joker hosts a successful late-night talk show. Some claim that he became a national celebrity because of his wacky Hoosier humor, which includes funding a scholarship for C students at Ball State. When Letterman's TV rating slipped, Indianapolis mayor Stephen Goldsmith knew why: "Clearly, his midwestern and Hoosier appeal has been affected by being out of the state too long."

HOOSIER HYSTERIA

Nothing excites Hoosiers more than sports. Whether professional or amateur, college or high school, hometown teams and races inspire crazy devotion—better known as "Hoosier hysteria"—from Hoosier viewers.

Actor James Dean poses with a friend back home in Fairmount.

On the Sunday before Memorial Day, 350,000 eager fans pack the Indianapolis Motor Speedway for the world's most famous long-distance automobile race, the Indianapolis 500. Average car speeds were once seventy-five miles an hour. Today, death-defying speeds exceed two hundred miles per hour.

At one time, drivers were all men. In 1977, Janet Guthrie made car-racing history as the first woman to race in the Indy 500. In 1978 she raced again, this time placing ninth. But it took until 1992 for another woman, Lynn St. James, to qualify. St. James finished eleventh and was chosen Rookie of the Year, an honor once reserved for men.

Besides car racing, Indianapolis is home to the state's professional teams: the Pacers (basketball), Colts (football), Indianapolis Ice (hockey), and Indianapolis Indians (baseball), a minor league

Janet Guthrie at the Indy 500 in 1978.

"MAJOR" CYCLER

The capital's Major Taylor Velodrome is named for one of the fastest bicycle racers ever to compete. Marshall Taylor won his first race at age thirteen with a four-wheel cycle. The name "Major" came from his trick riding in military costume when he was a teenager. Although he often faced racism, Taylor became the fastest American short-distance rider. By 1899 he was the second black to win a world-class title. His speed and skill made him the most celebrated black athlete at the turn of the century.

team owned by the Montreal Expos. In addition, Indianapolis has Olympic-quality centers for swimming, wrestling, and cycling. The city regularly hosts big-name events like the 1994 World Rowing Championship.

The sports-crazed town is known as the "amateur sports capital," with more sports associations and Halls of Fame than any other city in the nation. As one reporter explained, "Indianapolis never met a sport it didn't like."

Depending on the season, Hoosiers root for Indiana University, Notre Dame, and Purdue football and basketball teams. Notre Dame's quarterback Joe Montana, kick returner Tim Brown, and famous coach Knute Rockne created national interest long before they entered the world of professional football.

Indiana University's basketball coach Bobby Knight and his temper at games make Hoosier headlines regularly. Back in 1979, Boston Celtics player Larry Bird was the highest-paid rookie in professional sports history. Yet Bird remains a local hero for his shots at Indiana State University in Terre Haute, where he led his team to the 1979 basketball finals. Hoosiers still call him the "Hick from

Celtic Larry Bird shoots a two-pointer over the Hawk's Tree Rollins. Bird led the Celtics to two NBA championships and earned the league's most valuable player title three times.

French Lick," a joking reminder of the town which he was raised.

Competition has always existed between big-city and country schools. But the real frenzy whips up around basketball. Of the 385 public and private high schools, only three are without boys' basketball teams and six have no girls' teams. In many small farm communities, the stadium is the largest building within miles. Fifteen of the country's sixteen largest gyms are in Indiana— including the nation's largest, a 9,314-seat hall in Newcastle.

In Indiana, high school basketball is more like religion. Entire towns close down for school basketball games. The high school basketball game is one time when small towns can compete with big-city Hoosiers and possibly win—or at least it was until 1996. That's when the Indiana High School Athletic Association ended the eighty-five-year-old system of having all teams play in a single league. Instead, the association sorted the state's 382 teams into four tournaments by school size.

Fans were deeply divided. Many agreed that the divisions might benefit smaller schools. With fewer talented players to choose from and less money to spend, these schools tended to lose games repeatedly. As one fourteen-year-old basketball player said, "I'd rather be winning."

Older Hoosiers proudly referred to Milan's 1954 win over Muncie, a school fifteen times Milan's size. Five Milan boys started their careers shooting balls into peach baskets and went on to become state champions. Milan's lucky season sparked the movie *Hoosiers*.

"Everyone says Milan was 40 years ago," said Larry Bundy. Bundy played for Knightstown, a school of 404 students, over 35 years ago and doesn't miss a sectional game. "To me, there's a Milan every year because almost each season a small school gets to the Sweet 16 [sectional], and everyone is pulling for them." Now that's Hoosier pride!

6 HOOSIER HIGHLIGHTS

"The Narrows" covered bridge near Turkey Run State Park

Indiana is one of those places where a city named South Bend is in the north part of the state and North Vernon is in the south. And towns in Indiana flatlands are named after mountainous locations like Peru and Geneva. The oddest name is Santa Claus. The town's post office receives half a million letters each December addressed to the red-suited, bearded legend.

Another puzzle is the number of places with the same name. For example, Indiana claims four Buena Vistas and four Salems. There are even two Pumpkin Centers.

State highways connect most good-sized cities. Still, finding unusual hideaways can be tricky. This is no hardship for visitors, though. From south to north, Hoosiers befriend travelers—whether they are lost or not.

Hoosierland is a blend of rough industrial cities and quiet farm communities. But whatever the size, Indiana cities look and feel like small towns.

THE SOUTH

The town of Columbus is an architectural marvel. Plopped between Brown County log cabins and flat midwestern farmland are more than fifty buildings by the world's finest architects. The First Christian Church was designed by top architect Eliel Saarinen in 1942.

PLACES TO SEE

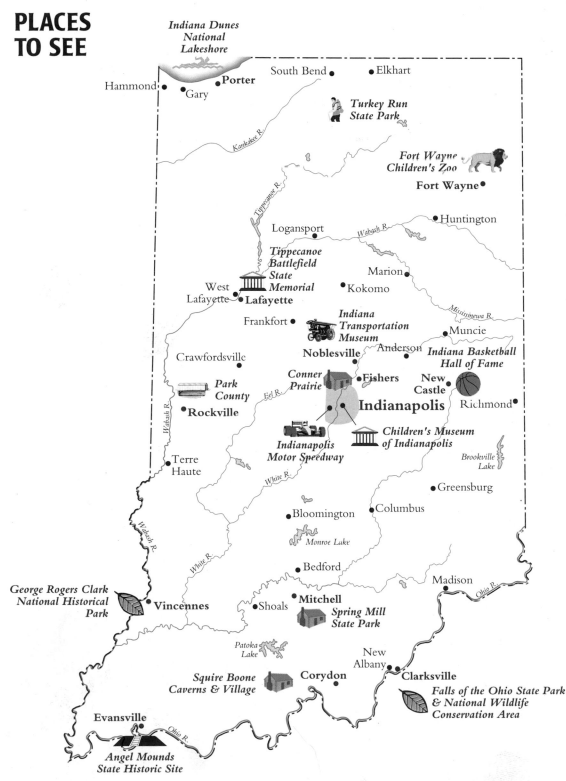

Indiana Dunes National Lakeshore

Hammond
Gary
Porter
South Bend
Elkhart

Turkey Run State Park

Kankakee R.

Fort Wayne Children's Zoo
Fort Wayne

Tippecanoe R.

Huntington

Logansport
Wabash R.

Tippecanoe Battlefield State Memorial
Marion
West Lafayette
Lafayette
Kokomo
Mississinewa R.

Frankfort
Indiana Transportation Museum
Noblesville
Anderson
Muncie
Indiana Basketball Hall of Fame

Crawfordsville

Park County
Conner Prairie
Fishers
New Castle
Rockville
Eel R.
Indianapolis
Richmond

Indianapolis Motor Speedway
Children's Museum of Indianapolis
Wabash R.
Brookville Lake
Terre Haute
White R.

Greensburg

Bloomington
Columbus

Monroe Lake

White R.
Bedford
Madison
Ohio R.

George Rogers Clark National Historical Park
Vincennes
Shoals
Mitchell
Spring Mill State Park

Patoka Lake
New Albany

Squire Boone Caverns & Village
Corydon
Clarksville
Falls of the Ohio State Park & National Wildlife Conservation Area

Evansville
Ohio R.
Angel Mounds State Historic Site

At the time, its clean lines revolutionized American church design. Fifteen years later, the Cummins Engine Foundation agreed to pay leading architects to plan new public buildings and preserve old treasures.

Architectural Wonders. City leaders have adopted the motto that anything "worth building is worth building right." Now structures by design greats Harry Weese, Eero Saarinen (Eliel's son), Richard Meier, and I. M. Pei dot the city's skyline. Schools, fire stations, factories, even the county jail have bold shapes and lively colors. Sculptures by Henry Moore, Jean Tinguely, Constantino Nivola, and Robert Indiana—a proud Hoosier who took the state's name—enhance building plazas, riverfront parks, and shopping areas. Visitors from around the world herald Coumbus as "America's architectural showplace" and "Athens of the prairie."

Columbus's respect for architecture has embraced the fine arts and the variety of ethnic groups that create them. The town of about thirty-five thousand people supports an arts center, a dance company, theater productions, and the state's oldest symphony orchestra. Unlike some Indiana towns, Columbus is set on building a community "open to every race, color, and opinion."

"This group of people really cares about the community and its development," noted the architect Richard Meier. "It uses the best talent . . . for the good of the citizens."

Rooted in the Past. Other areas of southern Indiana remain steeped in history. A visit to Vincennes, Indiana's first town, and the restored buildings in New Harmony is like stepping into the past. Vincennes preserves Grouseland, the home of the first Indiana Territory governor and ninth president of the United States,

Visitors can wander through the rooms of Grouseland, William Henry Harrison's home, and stroll down the streets of Vincennes, Indiana's first town.

William Henry Harrison. Nearby is Elihu Stout's print shop, the first in the Northwest Territory, complete with copies of the earliest *Indiana Gazette*.

Since 1920, the same fifty-cent toll bridge has connected New Harmony with Illinois. The town's ivy-covered buildings look as they did in the 1800s when they were built. The nation's first golden raintrees, brought here by German pioneers, edge narrow brick streets. Their unusual leafed trunks remain as green as grass, even in winter. In the third week of June, they burst into bloom and then shed their petals in a shower of brilliant gold.

"We still follow many German traditions," explains Velma Fisher. "Each Christmas we hide a glass pickle ornament on the tree, as our ancestors did. The person who finds the pickle receives an extra present." Townspeople also celebrate their roots during the annual Golden Raintree Festival, Heritage Week, and Kunstfest (arts festival).

Exploring Outdoors. "I happen to like country and woods and land with open space. I fell in love with southern Indiana," a Massachusetts-born Hoosier recalls.

Southern Indiana has many lovely spots. Madison and Newburgh are nestled in the Ohio River valley. Both picture-perfect towns recall Indiana's steamboat days. A tour of Madison includes a visit to homes once owned by riverboat captains and railroad barons. In Newburgh, houses along the water still have captain's walks, where seamen kept a lookout for their boats.

To the west is the rugged country of Abraham Lincoln and Squire Boone. The Lincoln Boyhood Natural Memorial is a model of the village where Abe lived as a boy, complete with a working 160-acre farm and museum. "Abraham, very large for his age, had an axe put into his hand at once; and from that moment till well into his twenty-third year, he was almost constantly handling the most useful instrument," wrote a biographer of Lincoln's Indiana days.

Squire Boone and his brother Daniel discovered awesome below-ground cave formations and waterfalls in 1790. Squire stayed to build a gristmill powered by water from the caverns. In 1973 the mill and village he founded were restored and turned into a living museum. But the greatest fun is trekking through the secret underground passageways.

"Indiana's state park system is one of the finest in the nation," claims Purdue professor Harry Targ.

This cabin at the two-hundred-acre Lincoln State Park looks like the one Abraham Lincoln grew up in with his older sister Sarah, father Thomas, and stepmother Sara Bush Johnston. As an adult Lincoln recalled fondly how Sara raised him from age nine after his mother died. "All that I am, or hope to be, I owe to my angel Mother."

Four of the six park inns are in the south. At these resorts, nature lovers can hike, swim, and bird-watch. Waterfalls, rolling hills, and caverns are scattered throughout Hoosier National Forest. Intriguing finds are everywhere—from Bedford's limestone quarries to the charm of Brown County.

Clifty Falls is called "one of Indiana's greatest beauty spots." High bluffs, deep canyons, and beech and maple woods surround the waterways in this 1,360-acre state park near Madison.

CENTRAL INDIANA

Indianapolis is unusual among the nation's large cities. It prospered even though its nearby waterways were too shallow for steamboat travel. Once people called the state capital India-No-Place. Today Indianapolis hums with government, business, sports, and cultural activities.

Ringing the Capital. The hub of Indianapolis is Mile Square. In 1820 surveyor Alexander Ralston planned the capital with a mile-square center. A wide street circled the timbered hill. Main roads extended from the circle like spokes on a wheel.

Today the rise is called Monument Circle. Here sits the 284-foot Soldiers and Sailors Monument, a city landmark. The limestone structure, indoor museum, and surrounding statues remember Hoosier soldiers who fought in the Mexican, Civil, and Spanish-American Wars.

A recent project to remodel government and office buildings helped Mile Square blossom. In 1996, Circle Centre and the Indianapolis Artsgarden, a retail and entertainment complex, opened. Streets were repaved, trees planted, and period lights installed. Downtown workers renovated old apartments and converted warehouses into lofts and studios. Cafés, department stores, and art galleries opened downtown to serve the new city dwellers.

Not far away is Union Station, the last midwestern Victorian-style train station. The station was turned into an indoor carnival of stores, restaurants, and entertainment that connects with the Pacers' Market Square Arena. Nearby is RCA Dome, where the Colts play football. Its nineteen-story dome is inflated with air from twenty electric fans.

Indianapolis city lights shine on the thirty-eight-foot-tall bronze statue, Victory, *crowning the Soldiers and Sailors Monument. Hoosiers call the statue "Miss Indiana."*

The arts have mushroomed in Indianapolis as well. The new Circle Theater houses the Indianapolis Symphony Orchestra. The Indiana Repertory Theatre stages plays in a renovated movie palace. The Indianapolis Opera Company performs to sellout crowds at the city's Murat Theatre. And the Madam Walker Urban Life Center offers African-American theater and jazz concerts in a building that once housed Walker's beauty products empire.

North of Monument Circle is the Children's Museum, the largest hands-on playground in the world. Visitors can wind through a limestone cave, ride an old-fashioned carousel, explore an Egyptian tomb, and travel into space. Museum developers wanted a place "where children grow up and adults don't have to."

In 1977, Indianapolis began developing White River State Park. Eleven years later, the Indianapolis Zoo opened here with two thousand animals. Today the zoo features camel rides, an indoor desert setting for reptiles, and dolphin shows.

At the entrance to the park is the Eiteljorg Museum. Its large collection of paintings from the American West and of Native American handiwork is unique in the Midwest. The building's large round base and red cedar canopy represent a kiva, the sacred space in Indian pueblo communities.

A life-sized, thirty-five-foot-long model of Tyrannosaurus rex guards the Children's Museum of Indianapolis.

Indianapolis's real fame comes from the Indianapolis 500, held in May. Anytime of year, however, the Speedway Museum Hall of Fame, located in the center of the track, displays trophies, helmets, photos, and racing cars. Young and old can feel the thrill of the race by circling the track on a bus tour or by climbing into cars that belonged to famous drivers.

East of Capital City. Ten miles east of Marion County in Greenfield is the birthplace of poet James Whitcomb Riley. The ten-room frame house pays tribute to the man who recorded nineteenth-century Indiana at its best. The porch view reveals the setting that must have triggered Riley's lively imagination. This was the same porch where "Little Orphant Annie" warned the children,

> "An' the Gobble-uns 'at gits you
> Ef you
> Don't
> Watch
> Out!"

"Everybody knows that Conner Prairie is one of the best, most realistic living museums in the country," exclaims traveler Richard Benjamin.

Conner Prairie is four miles south of Noblesville, past the Camel Lot with llamas, tigers, and zebras. The pioneer village recalls the days when William Conner was an Indian trader and Hamilton County's earliest white settler. Men, women, and children in knee britches and long skirts reenact life in Prairietown, the 1836 historic village. Dressed as schoolmarms, carpenters, and blacksmiths, they teach school, work with wood, and pound heated iron to forge

Folks at Conner Prairie Pioneer Village dress and speak like early settlers. They weave baskets, chop wood, and make candles for indoor light. Teachers scold students who slouch on their bench seat, chew gum, or talk out of turn. Even modern-day offenders must stand with their nose touching a circle on the chalkboard to remind them of their misdeeds.

tools. Visitors can see how pioneers made candles and soap, played dulcimers, and wove cloth.

Covered Bridge Country. The hills and forested ravines of Putnam County open onto the flat farmland of west-central Indiana. This is Parke County, known for maple syrup, mushrooms, and, most of all, covered bridges. Thirty-three covered bridges cross the region's many zigzagging streams. That's more

PARKE COUNTY HAUNTED BRIDGE

Legend says that Leatherwood Station (no. 25) covered bridge in Parke County is haunted. Once, as a girl and her uncle approached the bridge, they heard a buggy racing toward them from the other side. The uncle stopped his buggy, and they waited. The hoofbeats grew louder and faster, but no buggy appeared. Then the sounds stopped suddenly. After a few minutes, the pair drove through the empty bridge—too scared to talk about what had happened.

covered bridges than in any other county in the country!

All but ten of Parke County's bridges are still safe for travel. The longest single-lane covered bridge in the world crosses a winding stream in Turkey Run State Park. Three rebuilt bridges have been moved to Billie Creek Village in Rockville. The town is at the center of Parke County's ten-day Covered Bridge Festival, held in October, when the bridges are framed by the brilliant colors of fall.

NORTHERN INDIANA

In 1821, John Tipton surveyed the region along the shores of Lake Michigan. He noted afterward that he doubted the area "would ever be of much service to our state." Not true, said Octave Chanute. He conducted the first glider experiments from these secluded sand dunes. Chanute's 1896 flight in a heavier-than-air machine inspired Millville-born Wilbur Wright and his brother, Orville, to build their own plane four years later.

Dunes and Smokestacks. Today the region is packed with steel mills, marinas, shopping malls, and neighborhoods of small homes. City dwellers come from as far away as Chicago to pick blueberries, peaches, and apples in Porter County orchards. Beyond the fruit farms lies the second busiest national park east of the Rocky Mountains.

Indiana Dunes National Lakeshore is a year-round haven for sports fans and nature lovers. There are hiking and biking trails, beaches, and a nature center. Campgrounds are open in summer and cross-country ski trails run through the snow in winter. The Paul Douglas Center for Environmental Education houses programs for children throughout the year.

Fort Wayne. Fort Wayne, Indiana's second largest city, is a major industrial center. Its population of 173,000 supports almost four hundred factories. Even though business comes first in Fort Wayne, people still make time to relax. And the city has some outstanding showplaces.

"Fort Wayne is in the heart of soybean country," says an out-of-stater. "But it's got this old wooden fort in town, which is neat."

Historic Fort Wayne is an exact copy of the original 1816 military fort. Actors dressed in period clothes go about their nineteenth-century business. They perform military exercises and everyday chores like baking bread, smoking meat, and shaping hot iron into horseshoes.

Fort Wayne's Lincoln Museum contains the world's largest private collection of paintings, letters, and photographs about the sixteenth president. A library contains ten thousand books about Abraham Lincoln in twenty-six languages. Many objects on display came from Lincoln's offspring. Lincoln's son Robert Todd gave the museum the photograph of his father that appears on the five-dollar bill. The museum bought more pictures in 1985, after the death of Robert Beckwith, Lincoln's great-grandson and last living relative.

Fort Wayne's Children's Zoo may be small, but it receives worldwide applause for its landscaping and exhibit design. The Australian wildlife exhibit contains a twenty-thousand-gallon Great Barrier Reef aquarium, the largest on the North American continent. Visitors delight in watching more than five hundred animals from every part of the world in thirty-eight habitats.

Science Central is a special Indiana museum. The aim here is to have fun with science and math. Hands-on exhibits invite children and adults to walk on the moon, drop from a parachute, or ride a high-rail bike twenty feet off the ground. The museum even hosts summertime Camp Invention and a spring science carnival. At Science Central, children are told that it's okay to ask questions.

Clowning Around in Peru. From 1884 until 1930, seven major world circuses wintered near Peru, Indiana, an industrial community of fourteen thousand people. Thousands of people from miles around loved watching the performers and animals train. In 1958, townspeople decided to revive Peru's rich circus heritage with the Circus City Festival.

The first festival was small—a parade downtown and a few free acts on the courthouse lawn. Today almost two thousand people stage festival events for nearly forty thousand visitors. About 250 Miami County youngsters, age seven to twenty-one, perform all the acts. They tumble and fly on trapezes, high wires, and motorcycles, while "kiddie clowns" strut around the arena. The celebration ends with a huge parade of more than one hundred circus wagons and a fifty-piece band.

Teamwork plays a big part in performing awesome trapeze acts at Circus City Festival.

"These kids who perform learn other basics, like depending upon other people and getting along," adds Linda Cawood, Youth Circus coordinator. "They have something they are proud of the rest of their lives."

This pride seems to be a part of most Hoosiers. Those who move away carry a bit of Indiana with them. And those who move to the state settle in for good.

As transplanted New Yorker Irving Liebowitz wrote in *My Indiana*, "Here are proud people . . . full of noisy patriotism, perhaps, but ruggedly independent. This is where livin' is easy. I never had it so good."

THE FLAG: The Indiana state flag shows 19 gold stars, a gold torch, and the word "Indiana" in gold on a field of blue. The torch stands for liberty and enlightenment. The 13 stars in the outer circle represent the original 13 states. The 5 stars in the lower inner circle represent the next 5 states to be admitted to the union. The large star above the torch stands for Indiana.

THE SEAL: The state seal shows a pioneer chopping down a tree with a bison running off in the foreground. The sun gleams over a hill in the background. The words "Seal of the State of Indiana" are found above the picture, and the year of Indiana statehood, 1816, is found below. The seal was officially adopted in 1963.

STATE SURVEY

Statehood: December 11, 1816

Origin of Name: Indiana means "land of the Indians." The state was named for the large number of Native Americans living there in the late eighteenth and early nineteenth centuries.

Nickname: Hoosier State

Capital: Indianapolis

Motto: Crossroads of America

Flower: Peony

Tree: Tulip tree

Bird: Cardinal

Stone: Indiana limestone

Tree peony

Cardinal

GEOGRAPHY

Highest Point: 1,257 feet above sea level near Bethel

Lowest Point: 320 feet above sea level along the Ohio River in Posey County

Area: 36,291 square miles

Greatest Distance North to South: 265 miles

ON THE BANKS OF THE WABASH, FAR AWAY

Composer Paul Dresser was born in Terre Haute, on the banks of the Wabash. He wrote his most famous song, "On the Banks of the Wabash," in 1899. Within a year of its composition it had sold over one million copies of sheet music—an amazing amount for this prephonograph era. In 1913 it was adopted as the official state song.

By Paul Dresser

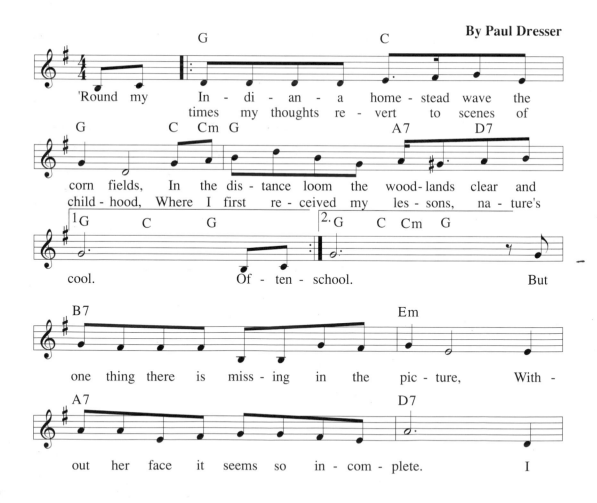

Greatest Distance East to West: 140 miles

Bordering States: Michigan to the north, Kentucky to the south, Ohio to the east, and Illinois to the west

Hottest Recorded Temperature: 116° F at Collegeville on July 14, 1936

Coldest Recorded Temperature: -36° F at New Whitehead on January 19, 1994

Average Annual Precipitation: 40 inches

Major Rivers: Big Blue, Calumet, Eel, Elkhart, Iroquois, Kankakee, Maumee, Ohio, Patoka, St. Joseph, Tippecanoe, Wabash, White, White-water

Major Lakes: Brookville, Freeman, Manitou, Maxinkuckee, Monroe, Patoka, Prairie Creek, Raccoon, Salamonie, Shafer, Tippecanoe, Wawasee

Trees: ash, hickory, maple, pecan, red oak, walnut, white oak, yellow poplar

Wild plants: aster, bladderwort, corn cockle, fringed gentian, golderod, iris, jack-in-the-pulpit, orchid, ox-eye daisy, peony, pitcher plant, prickly pear cactus, pussy willow, Queen Anne's lace, round-leaved sundew, sunflower, sweet clover, violet

Animals: beaver, fox, opossum, rabbit, raccoon, skunk, squirrel, weasel, white-tailed deer

Birds: bald eagle, bluebird, blue jay, cardinal, duck, horned owl, hummingbird, mourning dove, peregrine falcon, pileated woodpecker, quail, robin, ruffed grouse, swift, wild turkey

Peregrine Falcon

Fish: bass, bluegill, carp, catfish, crappie, perch, salmon, sunfish, trout

Endangered Animals: bald eagle, fat pocketbook pearly mussel, gray bat, Indiana bat, interior least tern, Kirtland's warbler, orange-foot pimple-back, peregrine falcon, pink mucket, piping plover, rough pigtoe, white cat's paw pearly mussel, white wartyback

Endangered Plants: mead's milkweed, pitcher's thistle, running buffalo clover

TIMELINE

Indiana History

c. 1000 B.C. Mound builders begin to develop communities in present-day Indiana

c. 1450 The large prehistoric structure at Angel Mounds stands empty

1679 French explorer René-Robert Cavalier, sieur de La Salle journeys down the St. Joseph River to the site of modern-day South Bend

1732 Indiana's oldest permanent community is established at Vincennes by the French

1751 The Miami leader Little Turtle is born at the site of present-day Fort Wayne

1754 The French and Indian War begins in which the French and British battle for control of the fur trade

1763 All of present-day Indiana becomes part of the British Empire as the French and Indian War ends with a British victory; British forts in Indiana are captured by Native Americans during Pontiac's Rebellion

1775–1783 The American Revolution is fought

1779 A force of Americans under George Rogers Clark captures Vincennes from the British

1787 Indiana becomes part of the Northwest Territory, an area that will eventually become five states

1791 Troops under General Arthur St. Clair are ambushed by Native Americans led by Little Turtle; the Americans lose over six hundred men

1794 After defeating a Native American force at the Battle of Fallen Timbers, fought on the Maumee River in Ohio, General Anthony Wayne moves up the Maumee and builds Fort Wayne

1800 The Indiana Territory is created with its capital at Vincennes

1809 In a treaty signed at Fort Wayne, territorial governor William Henry Harrison receives some 3 million acres from various Native American groups in Indiana

1811 Troops commanded by William Henry Harrison, who became the ninth president, defeat Native Americans in the Battle of Tippecanoe

1812 The War of 1812 begins

1816 Indiana becomes the nineteenth state

1816 The family of seven-year-old Abraham Lincoln moves from Kentucky to Indiana

1824 Indianapolis becomes the capital of Indiana

1825 Followers of Robert Owen come to New Harmony and found the state's first free school, free kindergarten, and coeducational school

1832 Construction of the Wabash and Erie Canal begins at Fort Wayne

1845 John "Johnny Appleseed" Chapman dies and is buried at Fort Wayne

1861–1865 The Civil War rages between the North and the South

1863 Confederate general John Morgan and 2,500 troops raid southern Indiana

1888 Benjamin Harrison is elected president of the United States

1917 The United States enters World War I; 130,670 Hoosiers serve in the armed forces during the war

1941 The United States enters World War II; about 338,000 Hoosiers serve in the war

1949 School desegregation is ordered by Indiana's general assembly

1967 Richard Hatcher is elected the state's first African-American mayor in Gary

1988 Dan Quayle, senator from Indiana, becomes vice president of the United States

ECONOMY

Agricultural Products: apples, cattle, chickens, corn, dairy products, eggs, hay, hogs, popcorn, oats, rye, soybeans, tobacco, tomatoes, turkeys, wheat

Manufactured Products: agricultural and industrial chemicals, aircraft parts, automobile parts, communications equipment, electrical instruments, farm machinery, iron and steel, musical instruments, other metals, processed foods, travel trailers and campers, wood cabinets

Natural Resources: bituminous coal, cement, clay, crushed stone, gypsum, iron slag, lime, limestone, natural gas, oil, peat, sand and gravel, timber

Business and Trade: communications, insurance, real estate, transportation, wholesale and retail sales

CALENDAR OF CELEBRATIONS

James Dean Birthday Celebration Every February, actor James Dean's hometown of Fairmount celebrates his birthday with a free showing of one of his films along with refreshments.

Maple Sugar Time See how sap is collected and turned into maple syrup at this March festival in Merrillville. There are movies and tours and pure maple syrup and candy to buy.

Mountain Men Rendezvous Held in April at Bridgeton, this festival re-creates a gathering of Indiana frontiersmen. You can buy authentic crafts displayed on the blankets of the mountain men and listen to stories told by the campfire.

Spirit of Vincennes Rendezvous Soldiers and battles of the Revolutionary War are the focus of this May festival. Watch reenactments of Revolutionary battles, listen to fife and drum corps, or taste foods prepared as they were in the 1700s.

Indiana State Pickin' and Fiddlin' Contest Hear the state's best on guitar, banjo, harmonica, and fiddle at this June festival in Petersburg. You can also listen to old-time singers and bluegrass bands.

Clay City Pottery Festival In June you can tour the only working stoneware pottery works in Indiana at Clay City and see how the pottery is made. The festival also displays crafts, antique cars, and tractors.

Woodland Nations Powwow The Miami people of Indiana host this June event in Muncie. Native American music, foods, and crafts are all a part of this weekend celebration.

Indiana Avenue Jazz Heritage Festival Held in August in Indianapolis, this festival features local and national jazz musicians. You can find lots of food, arts and crafts, and even a showcase for young musicians.

Watermelon Festival Brownstown celebrates their favorite summer treat in this August festival. There are crafts and entertainment, plenty of watermelon, and, of course, a seed-spitting contest.

Ligonier Marshmallow Festival This eastern Indiana town lays claim to the world's largest marshmallow. Crafts, food, parades, and rides can be found at this September festival.

Feast of the Hunters' Moon This weekend festival at Fort Ouiatenon Historic Park in Lafayette celebrates the life of Indiana's early French traders and Native Americans. You can see crafts, costumes, and games—including tomahawk-throwing contests—during this late September/early October festival.

Feast of the Hunters' Moon

Covered Bridge Festival Every October during this celebration, you can pick up a map in Rockville and drive to see the area's beautiful covered bridges and fall colors. There are also arts and crafts, music, and local foods like sweet corn and funnel cakes.

International Festival You can learn about cultures from all around the world at this festival held in Indianapolis in October. There are plenty of ethnic foods to taste as well as ethnic entertainment.

Festival of Gingerbread Everybody from children to professionals can compete in a gingerbread decorating contest at this Fort Wayne festival. Held in late November and early December, the celebration also features caroling and holiday lights.

STATE STARS

John "Johnny Appleseed" Chapman (1774–1847) is famous for his travels through the Ohio, Indiana, and Illinois Territories, where he planted numerous apple orchards. Chapman is buried in Fort Wayne.

Larry Bird (1956–   ) is one of basketball's all-time great players. Born in French Lick, Bird played pro basketball for thirteen years with the Boston Celtics and made basketball's All-Star Team twelve times.

Frank Borman (1928–   ) of Gary was one of the first three astronauts to orbit the moon. Borman served as the commander of that famous Apollo mission in 1968. He had also flown an earlier Gemini space mission.

Johnny Appleseed

Mordecai "Three Finger" Brown (1876–1948) was born in Nyesville. Although he had lost half a finger in a childhood accident, he went on to become a famous major league pitcher. Between 1906 and 1911, he averaged more than twenty wins a season for the Chicago Cubs. In 1949 Brown was named to the Baseball Hall of Fame.

Hoagland "Hoagy" Carmichael (1899 1981) is one of America's best loved songwriters. Born in Bloomington, Carmichael attended Indiana University. His hit songs included "Stardust" and "Georgia on My Mind."

William Merritt Chase (1849–1916), a famous American painter, was born in Nineveh. Chase founded the New York School of Art and painted landscapes and portraits of wealthy Americans.

Schuyler Colfax (1823–1885) served as vice president under Ulysses S. Grant from 1869 to 1873. Born in New York, Colfax moved to South Bend as a boy. He served in Congress as a representative from Indiana before becoming vice president.

Jim Davis (1945–   ), the creator of everybody's favorite cartoon cat, Garfield, was born in Marion. Garfield appears in some five hundred newspapers and also had his own Saturday morning television show.

James Dean (1931–1955) of Marion had a promising movie-acting career, which was cut short by a tragic car accident. Dean starred in *East of Eden*, *Rebel without a Cause*, and *Giant*.

Eugene V. Debs (1855–1926) of Terre Haute was a powerful American labor leader. Debs formed the American Railway

Eugene Debs

Union and supported one of the first large-scale strikes in the United States, the Pullman strike. In 1894, railway workers across the United States went on strike in support of workers at the Pullman Company in Chicago, which built railroad cars. Debs also ran for U.S. president five times.

Bob Griese (1945–   ) is one of football's best-known quarterbacks. Born in Evansville, Griese played college football at Purdue then led the Miami Dolphins to Super Bowl victories in 1973 and 1974.

Benjamin Harrison (1833–1901) was the twenty-third president of the United States. Born in Ohio, Harrison moved to Indianapolis as a young man and is buried there, in Crown Hill Cemetery. He was the grandson of the ninth president, William Henry Harrison.

Benjamin Harrison

William Henry Harrison (1773–1841) served as governor of the Indiana Territory and then as the ninth president of the United States. Harrison died from pneumonia after only a month in office.

Richard Hatcher (1933–   ) of Michigan City was one of the first African-American mayors of a large American city. Hatcher served as mayor of Gary from 1967 to 1987.

Jimmy Hoffa (1913–1975?) was born in the town of Brazil. A famous labor leader, Hoffa served as president of the Teamsters Union from 1958 to 1971. Hoffa mysteriously disappeared in 1975 and is believed to have been murdered.

Jimmy Hoffa

Michael Jackson (1958–   ) and his singing brothers and sisters were born in Gary. Michael was only ten years old when he had a hit record as the lead singer for the Jackson Five. As a solo artist, Jackson gained superstar status, and his album *Thriller* became the best-selling album of all time.

David Letterman (1947–   ), late night TV's wackiest talk-show host, was born in Indianapolis. Letterman went to Ball State University and began his showbiz career as a radio and television announcer in his hometown. He has won a number of Emmies for his popular talk show.

Little Turtle (1751–1812) was a respected leader of the Miami people of Indiana. Little Turtle led several victorious attacks against U.S. troops before he was defeated in the Battle of Fallen Timbers in 1794. He was born near the Eel River.

John Cougar Mellencamp (1951–   ), singer and songwriter, was born in Seymore. His pop songs often tell of small-town life. Mellencamp's hits include "Jack and Diane" and "Scarecrow."

Robert Dale Owen (1801–1877) was an Indiana politician and social reformer. As a member of the U.S. Congress, Owen helped found the Smithsonian Institution. He also helped establish Indiana's free school system. Owen's letter to President Lincoln in 1862 played a part in Lincoln's decision to emancipate America's slaves.

Cole Porter (1891–1964) was a songwriter whose hits include "Night and Day" and "I've Got You under My Skin." He also wrote many musicals including *Kiss Me, Kate*. He was born in Peru.

Gene Stratton Porter (1868–1924) was a writer of nature books and fictional works. Her novels *Freckles* and *The Girl of the Limberlost* were about life in the Limberlost marsh area of northern Indiana where she lived.

Dan Quayle

James Danforth Quayle (1947–) served as vice president of the United States from 1989 to 1993 under President George Bush. Born in Indianapolis, Quayle was a U.S. representative and senator from Indiana before becoming vice president.

James Whitcomb Riley (1849–1916), the "Hoosier Poet," was born in Greenfield. Riley's poetry was written in simple language and appealed to a large number of readers. His works included "The Old Swimmin' Hole," "Little Orphant Annie," and "The Raggedy Man."

Oscar Robertson (1938–) is a basketball standout from Indianapolis. At Crispus Attucks High School, Robertson helped his team become the first in Indiana history to have an unbeaten season. He was on the gold-medal-winning U.S. Olympic team in 1960, then went on to play pro ball for the Cincinnati Royals and the Milwaukee Bucks.

Knute Rockne (1888–1931) gained fame as a football coach for his exciting style of play and his winning record. As the coach at Notre Dame from 1918 to 1931, Rockne lost only twelve games while winning 105.

Red Skelton (1913–) won fame as a comedian playing a number of zany characters such as Clem Kadiddlehopper and Freddie the Free-loader. Skelton entertained on radio and television and in the movies. He was born in Vincennes.

Clement (1831–1901) and **John** (1833–1917) **Studebaker** were brothers who began making carriages in South Bend in the mid-1800s. The company started producing electric vehicles in 1902 and gasoline automobiles in 1904.

Tecumseh (1768–1813), a great Shawnee leader, who hoped to drive white settlers from the Indiana region. He gathered a force of Native Americans at a village on the Tippecanoe River, only to have his force defeated by an American army while Tecumseh, himself, was away.

Kurt Vonnegut, Jr. (1922–   ) uses fantasy to tell of the darker side of human life in his novels. His works include *Slaughterhouse Five* and *Breakfast of Champions*. Vonnegut was born in Indianapolis.

Sarah Breedlove Walker (1867–1919) moved to Indianapolis in 1910. Known as Madam C. J. Walker, she founded a company that made hair care products for African-American women. Walker became the first black woman millionaire.

Sarah Breedlove Walker

TOUR THE STATE

Fort Wayne's Children's Zoo (Fort Wayne) Exhibits at this zoo include the Indonesian Rain Forest, Orangutan Valley, and the Australian Adventure. The zoo also has the world's only Endangered Species Carousel.

Lincoln Museum (Fort Wayne) Exhibits depict Lincoln's life from his childhood in Indiana to his presidency. Using computers, visitors can read Lincoln's mail, fight a Civil War battle, or take a history quiz.

Historic Fort Wayne (Fort Wayne) The log buildings here look as they would have in 1816. Visitors can learn about the life of soldiers at the old fort and view artifacts that belonged to General Anthony Wayne and the Miami chief Little Turtle.

Circus City Festival Museum (Peru) The history of the circus is celebrated at this museum. Posters, costumes, and other circus-related items are on display.

Levi Coffin House State Historic Site (Fountain City) The home of Levi and Katherine Coffin was known as the "Grand Central Station of the underground railroad." More than two thousand enslaved people escaping from the South passed through the Coffin home.

Indiana Basketball Hall of Fame (New Castle) The history of Indiana basketball is featured at this museum. Displays honor state championship teams and superstars like Larry Bird.

Conner Prairie (Fishers) Life in an early 1800s Indiana village is the focus of this living-history museum. Costumed employees demonstrate everyday activities in the village's schoolhouse, general store, blacksmith shop, and other period buildings.

The Children's Museum of Indianapolis (Indianapolis) This exciting museum offers everything from life-size Tyrannosaurus rex to a limestone cave to an 1800s carousel. Space travel, world history, and nature are just a few of the subjects explored in this museum.

Eiteljorg Museum of American Indian and Western Art (Indianapolis) Cowboys and Indians and the American West are featured at this Indianapolis museum. Sculptures and paintings from famous Western artists and artwork from Native American cultures—such as clothing, baskets, and pottery—can be viewed here.

Indianapolis Motor Speedway (Indianapolis) Visitors to the world's most famous race track can see a film on the history of the Indianapolis 500, take a bus tour of the track, and explore the displays at the speedway's museum, which include Indy cars, objects belonging to famous drivers, and antique automobiles.

The Falls of the Ohio State Park and National Wildlife Conservation Area (Clarksville) Visitors to this park can view a fossil bed containing corals and other examples of prehistoric ocean life that are at least 400 million years old. There is a film on the history of the falls in the visitor center and a wildlife observation center.

Spring Mill State Park (Mitchell) A water-powered gristmill, sawmill, post office, and boot shop are among the buildings of this reconstructed 1815 village. There is also a memorial to astronaut Virgil I. Grissom, an Indiana native, which includes a space capsule and a presentation on space exploration.

Squire Boone Caverns and Village (Corydon) The sparkling underground rock formations and waterways at this site were first discovered by Daniel Boone and his brother Squire in 1790. Pioneer crafts are demonstrated in the village's log cabins.

*Lincoln Boyhood
National Memorial*

Lincoln Boyhood National Memorial (Lincoln City) The farm where Lincoln lived between 1816 and 1830 is preserved at this site. Visitors can tour the reconstructed homestead, the visitor center, and the grave of Lincoln's mother.

Angel Mounds State Historic Site (Evansville) Once the location of a village of prehistoric mound-builders, the site today displays reconstructed dwellings and other buildings from A.D. 1200 to 1400.

Battle Ground Wolf Park (Lafayette) Visitors to this unique park can see wolves and bison interact much as they would in the wild. The wolves "hunt" the bison, although they are not allowed to harm them.

Tippecanoe Battlefield State Memorial (Lafayette) The site of William Henry Harrison's victory over Native Americans under the leadership of Tecumseh's brother, the Prophet, today has a museum to help explain the events surrounding the battle. The park also contains walking trails.

Indiana Dunes National Lakeshore (Porter) The ever-shifting dunes along Lake Michigan offer a number of ways to have fun. You can hike and swim, as well as explore a nineteenth-century farm and see exhibits on the area's plants and wildlife.

FIND OUT MORE

If you'd like to find out more about Indiana, look in your school library, local library, bookstore, or video store. Here are some titles:

STATE BOOKS

Berry, Skip. *Indianapolis*. Minneapolis, MN: Dillon Press, 1990.

Stein, Conrad. *America the Beautiful: Indiana*. Chicago: Childrens Press, 1990.

PEOPLE AND SPECIAL-INTEREST BOOKS

Bundles, A'Lelia Perry. *Madam C. J. Walker*. New York: Chelsea House, 1991.

Dolan, Sean. *Larry Bird*. New York: Chelsea House, 1995.

Henry, Joanne Landers. *Log Cabin in the Woods: A True Story About a Pioneer Boy*. New York: Macmillan, 1988.

Riley, James Whitcomb. *Little Orphant Annie*. G. P. Putnam: New York, 1983.

Stratton Porter, Gene. *A Girl of the Limberlost*. Grosset & Dunlap: New York, 1909.

VIDEOS

Breaking Away. 180 minutes. Farmington Hills, MI: Magnetic Video Corporation, 1979. (Bicycle race shows competition between small-town stonecutter boys and big-city college boys.)

Hoosiers. 115 minutes. Hemdale Film Corporation, 1986. Distributed by HBO Video, New York. (Emphasizes the importance of high school basketball to small-town Indiana.)

Indiana. 49 minutes. Milwaukee, WI: Raintree Publishing, 1994. (Five short segments show different Hoosier lifestyles.)

Rudy. 113 minutes. Burbank, CA: Columbia TriStar, 1994. (Hoosier boy follows his dream to become a Notre Dame football player, even though he has always been told that he is not good enough, smart enough, or big enough to play.)

CD-ROMS AND AUDIOTAPES

Human Wheels (sound CD), by John Cougar Mellencamp. New York: Mercury, 1993.

The Incredible Jazz Guitar (sound CD), by Wes Montgomery. New York: Verve Records, 1987.

Soulsation: 25th Anniversary Collection (sound CD), by the Jackson Five. Los Angeles: Motown, 1995. (Gary family of talented Jacksons, including Michael Jackson.)

Where in the World Is Carmen Sandiego? (sound CD). New York: Zoom Express, BMG Kids, 1992. (Includes songs that highlight Indiana.)

INDEX

Page numbers for illustrations are in boldface.